BIG IDEAS MATH®
Geometry

Assessment Book

- Prerequisite Skills Test

- Pre-Course Test with Item Analysis

- Quiz

- Chapter Tests

- Alternative Assessment

- Performance Task

- Cumulative Test

- Post Course Test with Item Analysis

BIG IDEAS LEARNING®

Erie, Pennsylvania

Photo Credits

Cover Image Allies Interactive/Shutterstock.com

Printed in the United States

ISBN 13: 978-1-60840-856-6
ISBN 10: 1-60840-856-6

456789-VLP-18 17

Contents

About the Assessment Book

Prerequisite Skills Test with Item Analysis

The Prerequisite Skills Test checks students' understanding of previously learned mathematical skills they will need to be successful in Geometry. The Item Analysis can be used to determine topics that need to be reviewed.

Pre-Course Test with Item Analysis

Post Course Test with Item Analysis

The Pre-Course Test and Post Course Test cover key concepts that students will learn in their Geometry course. The Item Analysis can be used to determine topics that need to be reviewed.

Quiz

The Quiz provides ongoing assessment of student understanding. The quiz appears at the halfway point of the chapter.

Chapter Tests

The Chapter Tests provide assessment of student understanding of key concepts taught in the chapter. There are two tests for each chapter.

Alternative Assessment with Scoring Rubric

Each Alternative Assessment includes at least one multi-step problem that combines a variety of concepts from the chapter. Students are asked to explain their solutions, write about the mathematics, or compare and analyze different situations.

Performance Task

The Performance Task presents an assessment in a real-world situation. Every chapter has a task that allows students to work with multiple standards and apply their knowledge to realistic scenarios.

Cumulative Test

The Cumulative Test provides students practice answering questions in standardized test format. The assessments cover material from multiple chapters of the textbook. The questions represent problem types and reasoning patterns frequently found on standardized tests.

Name _____ Date _____

 Skills Test **Prerequisite Skills Test**

Simplify the expression.

Answers

1. $|3 - 7|$
2. $|-2 - 5|$
3. $|1 + (-8)|$

4. $|10 - (-7)|$
5. $|-6 + 5|$
6. $|2 + 12|$

7. $|-7 + (-4)|$
8. $|0 - 11|$
9. $|-2 - (-13)|$

Find the area of the triangle.

10.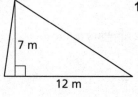
7 m
12 m

11.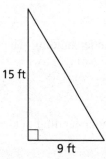
15 ft
9 ft

12.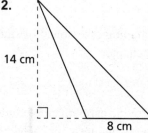
14 cm
8 cm

Write an equation for the *n*th term of the arithmetic sequence. Then find a_{40}.

13. 2, 4, 6, 8, …
14. −5, −1, 3, 7, …
15. 4.1, 5.6, 7.1, 8.6, …

16. 81, 72, 63, 54, …
17. 6, −1, −8, −15, …
18. $\frac{1}{4}, \frac{1}{2}, \frac{3}{4}, 1, …$

Solve the literal equation for *x*.

19. $3y = 3x + 1$
20. $3y - 4x = 12$

21. $2y - 6 = 5x + 8$
22. $2x + y = 6$

23. $y = zx - 2x + 5$
24. $z = 3x + 2xy$

Find the slope of the line.

25.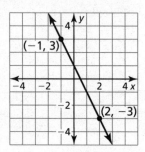
(−1, 3)
(2, −3)

Answers

1. _____
2. _____
3. _____
4. _____
5. _____
6. _____
7. _____
8. _____
9. _____
10. _____
11. _____
12. _____
13. _____
14. _____
15. _____
16. _____
17. _____
18. _____
19. _____
20. _____
21. _____
22. _____
23. _____
24. _____
25. _____

2 **Geometry**
Assessment Book

Name_____ Date_____

Find the slope of the line.

Answers

26.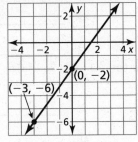

27.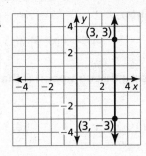

26. _____

27. _____

28. _____

29. _____

30. _____

31. _____

Write an equation of the line that passes through the given point and has the given slope.

28. $(1, 4)$; $m = -1$

29. $(-1, -5)$; $m = $ undefined

30. $(2, 3)$; $m = 3$

31. $(-5, 3)$; $m = 0$

32. $(-2, 1)$; $m = -\dfrac{5}{2}$

33. $(-4, -4)$; $m = \dfrac{1}{2}$

32. _____

33. _____

34. _____

35. _____

Tell whether the grey figure is a translation, reflection, rotation, or dilation of the black figure.

36. _____

37. _____

38. _____

34.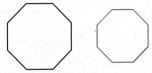

35.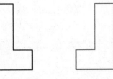

36.

37.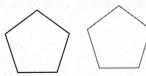

39. _____

_____

_____

Tell whether the two figures are similar. Explain your reasoning.

38.
```
      16
 ┌──────────┐
 │          │ 6
 └──────────┘
   ┌──────┐
   │      │ 3
   └──────┘
      8
```

39.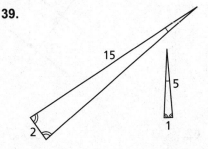

40. _____

41. _____

42. _____

Solve the equation.

40. $7x + 3 = 4x$

41. $13 - y = 12y$

42. $4m - 11 = 2m + 21$

43. $3w - 5 = -5w + 11$

44. $-x - 1 = -3x - 7$

45. $g - 10 = 8g - 10$

43. _____

44. _____

45. _____

Skills Test **Prerequisite Skills Test** (continued)

Find the midpoint *M* of the segment with the given endpoints. Then find the distance between the two endpoints.

46. $A(-4, 7)$ and $B(3, -1)$ 47. $A(0, 5)$ and $B(-3, -6)$

46. _____

_____

Write an equation of the line passing through point *P* that is perpendicular to the given line.

47. _____

48. $P(2, 4)$, $y = \frac{1}{2}x - 6$ 49. $P(6, 0)$, $y = 4$ 50. $P(-3, 4)$, $y = -\frac{2}{3}x$

_____

48. _____

Write the sentence as an inequality.

49. _____

51. A number x is greater than 6 but less than 10.

50. _____

52. A number y is at most 2 or at least 5.

51. _____

53. A number b is less than or equal to -4 or greater than 0.

52. _____

54. A number k is more than -7 and less than -1.

53. _____

Solve the equation by interpreting the expression in parentheses as a single quantity.

54. _____

55. $2(x + 5) = 12$ 56. $2 + 6(7 - x) = 20$

55. _____

57. $3(x - 2) + 7(x - 2) = 30$ 58. $-4 - 2(3 - x) = -2(x + 3)$

56. _____

57. _____

Determine which lines are parallel and which are perpendicular.

58. _____

59. 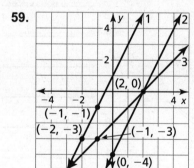 60.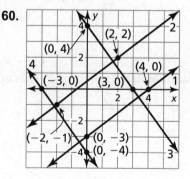

59. _____

60. _____

_____

61. _____

62. _____

Simplify the expression.

63. _____

61. $\sqrt{48}$ 62. $\sqrt{216}$ 63. $\sqrt{108}$

64. _____

65. _____

64. $\dfrac{5}{\sqrt{3}}$ 65. $\dfrac{8}{\sqrt{2}}$ 66. $\dfrac{10}{\sqrt{5}}$

66. _____

Name_____ Date_____

Tell whether the ratios form a proportion.

Answers

67. $\dfrac{6}{14}, \dfrac{9}{21}$ **68.** $\dfrac{15}{10}, \dfrac{10}{5}$ **69.** $\dfrac{16}{50}, \dfrac{24}{75}$

67. _____

68. _____

Solve the proportion.

69. _____

70. $\dfrac{4}{k} = \dfrac{2}{9}$ **71.** $\dfrac{2}{8} = \dfrac{5}{k-8}$ **72.** $\dfrac{3a+8}{6} = \dfrac{10}{8}$

70. _____

Find the product.

71. _____

73. $(x+4)(x+2)$ **74.** $(m-2)(m-5)$ **75.** $(x-1)(2+5x)$

72. _____

76. $(g+5)(4g-1)$ **77.** $(x+9)(x-9)$ **78.** $(1+3a)(5-2a)$

73. _____

74. _____

Solve the equation by completing the square. Round your answer to the nearest hundredth, if necessary.

75. _____

79. $m^2 + 20m + 64 = 0$ **80.** $y^2 + 8y - 64 = 3$

76. _____

81. $x^2 + 4x - 88 = -10$ **82.** $-m^2 + 2m = -35$

77. _____

78. _____

Find the surface area of the prism.

83.
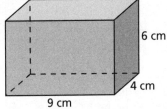
6 cm

4 cm

9 cm

79. _____

84.
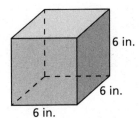
6 in.

6 in.

6 in.

80. _____

81. _____

82. _____

83. _____

85.
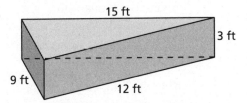
15 ft

3 ft

9 ft

12 ft

84. _____

85. _____

86. _____

Find the missing dimension.

87. _____

86. A rectangle has a perimeter of 68 meters and a length of 20 meters. What is the width of the rectangle?

88. _____

87. A triangle has an area of 58 square centimeters and a base of 8 centimeters. What is the height of the triangle?

88. A square has a perimeter of 24 feet. What is the length of the diagonal?

Prerequisite Skills Test Item Analysis

Item Number	Skills
1	finding absolute value
2	finding absolute value
3	finding absolute value
4	finding absolute value
5	finding absolute value
6	finding absolute value
7	finding absolute value
8	finding absolute value
9	finding absolute value
10	find the area of a triangle
11	find the area of a triangle
12	find the area of a triangle
13	finding the nth term of an arithmetic sequence
14	finding the nth term of an arithmetic sequence
15	finding the nth term of an arithmetic sequence
16	finding the nth term of an arithmetic sequence
17	finding the nth term of an arithmetic sequence
18	finding the nth term of an arithmetic sequence
19	rewriting literal equations
20	rewriting literal equations
21	rewriting literal equations
22	rewriting literal equations
23	rewriting literal equations
24	rewriting literal equations
25	finding the slope of a line

Item Number	Skills
26	finding the slope of a line
27	finding the slope of a line
28	writing equations of lines
29	writing equations of lines
30	writing equations of lines
31	writing equations of lines
32	writing equations of lines
33	writing equations of lines
34	identifying transformations
35	identifying transformations
36	identifying transformations
37	identifying transformations
38	identifying similar figures
39	identifying similar figures
40	solving equations with variables on both sides
41	solving equations with variables on both sides
42	solving equations with variables on both sides
43	solving equations with variables on both sides
44	solving equations with variables on both sides
45	solving equations with variables on both sides
46	using the Midpoint Formula and Distance Formula
47	using the Midpoint Formula and Distance Formula
48	writing an equation of a perpendicular line
49	writing an equation of a perpendicular line
50	writing an equation of a perpendicular line

Item Number	Skills
51	write an inequality
52	write an inequality
53	write an inequality
54	write an inequality
55	using structure to solve a multistep equation
56	using structure to solve a multistep equation
57	using structure to solve a multistep equation
58	using structure to solve a multistep equation
59	identifying parallel and perpendicular lines
60	identifying parallel and perpendicular lines
61	using properties of radicals
62	using properties of radicals
63	using properties of radicals
64	using properties of radicals
65	using properties of radicals
66	using properties of radicals
67	determining whether ratios form a proportion
68	determining whether ratios form a proportion
69	determining whether ratios form a proportion

Item Number	Skills
70	solving proportions
71	solving proportions
72	solving proportions
73	multiplying binomials
74	multiplying binomials
75	multiplying binomials
76	multiplying binomials
77	multiplying binomials
78	multiplying binomials
79	solving quadratic equations by completing the square
80	solving quadratic equations by completing the square
81	solving quadratic equations by completing the square
82	solving quadratic equations by completing the square
83	finding a surface area
84	finding a surface area
85	finding a surface area
86	finding a missing dimension
87	finding a missing dimension
88	finding a missing dimension

Name _____ Date _____

Find the length of $\overline{LN}$.

Answers

1.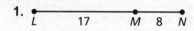

2.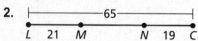

1. _____

2. _____

3. The endpoints of a line segment are $G(1, 7)$ and $H(-3, 11)$. Find the coordinates of the midpoint M. Find the distance between the endpoints of $\overline{GH}$.

3. _____

4. The midpoint of $\overline{GH}$ is $M(5, 7)$. One endpoint is $H(12, -9)$. Find the coordinates of endpoint G. Find the distance between the endpoints of $\overline{GH}$.

4. _____

Use the diagram to decide whether the statement is true or false.

5. Points A, B, and D are collinear.

5. _____

6. Plane Q and plane R intersect at line ℓ.

6. _____

7. Points E, D, and F lie in plane Q.

7. _____

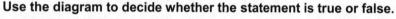

8. $\overrightarrow{AB}$ and $\overrightarrow{BD}$ are opposite rays.

8. _____

9. $\overrightarrow{AC}$ intersects $\overrightarrow{DE}$ at point B.

9. _____

10. Plane Q is perpendicular to plane R.

10. _____

Solve the equation.

11. _____

11. $7x + 25 = 13 + 3x$

12. $3(2x + 1) = -5x + 14$

12. _____

13. _____

Find the value of x. State which theorem you used.

13.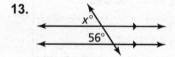

14.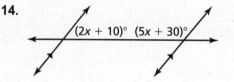

14. _____

15. _____

Find the value of x that makes $m \parallel n$.

16. _____

15.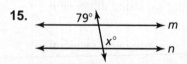

16.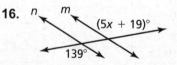

17. a._____

b._____

Write an equation of the line that passes through the given point and is (a) parallel to and (b) perpendicular to the given line.

18. a._____

b._____

17. $(-1, -5)$, $y = 2x - 4$

18. $(5, -2)$, $y = \frac{1}{5}x - 3$

Pre-Course **Pre-Course Test** (continued)

Graph △*RST* with vertices *R*(−2, 1), *S*(0, 4), and *T*(3, −2) and its image after the translation.

Answers

19. $(x, y) \rightarrow (x + 2, y - 1)$

20. $(x, y) \rightarrow (x - 3, y)$

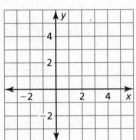

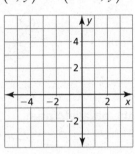

19. ____See left.____

20. ____See left.____

21. ____See left.____

22. ____See left.____

23. _____

_____

24. _____

_____

25. _____

26. _____

Graph the polygon with the given vertices and its image after a rotation of the given number of degrees about the origin.

21. *J*(3, 4), *F*(5, −2), *K*(1, −3); 90°

22. *G*(3, 2), *E*(3, 5), *O*(0, 2), *M*(−1, −2); 90°

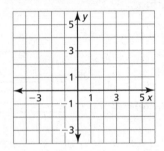

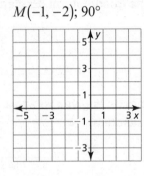

Find the measure of each acute angle.

23.

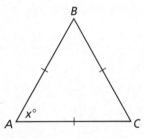

24.

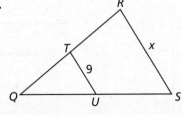

$\overline{TU}$ **is a midsegment of** △*QRS*. **Find the value of** *x*.

25.

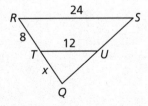

26.

Name _____ Date _____

Find *AC*. Identify the theorem you used.

Answers

27.

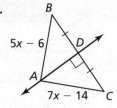

28.

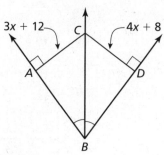

_____

_____

28. _____

_____

_____

29. _____

Find the value of each variable in the parallelogram.

29.

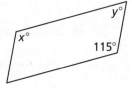

30.

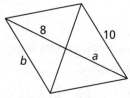

_____

_____

30. _____

_____

Give the most specific name for the quadrilateral. Explain your reasoning.

31.

32.

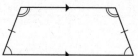

31. _____

_____

_____

_____

32. _____

Determine whether enough information is given to show that the quadrilateral is a parallelogram. Explain your reasoning.

33.

34.

_____

_____

33. _____

_____

_____

_____

Determine whether the triangles are similar. If they are, write a similarity statement.

35.

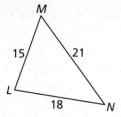

34. _____

_____

_____

35. _____

Find the value of the variable

36.

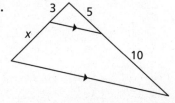

37.

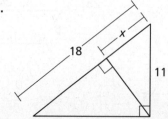

_____

36. _____

37. _____

Name_____ Date _____

Find the value of each variable. Round your answers to the nearest tenth.

Answers

38.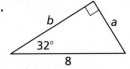

39.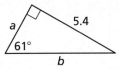

Find the measure of each numbered angle or arc in ⊙P.

40.

41.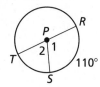

Find the value of the variable.

42.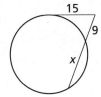

43.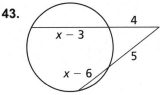

Find the volume of the solid.

44.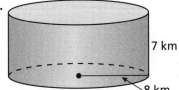

45.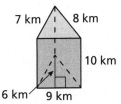

Find the indicated measure.

46. $m\overarc{AB}$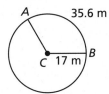

47. Area of shaded sector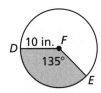

38. _____

_____

39. _____

_____

40. _____

_____

41. _____

_____

42. _____

43. _____

44. _____

45. _____

46. _____

47. _____

Pre-Course Test Item Analysis

Item Number	Skills
1	finding segment lengths
2	finding segment lengths
3	using Midpoint Formula and Distance Formula
4	using Midpoint Formula and Distance Formula
5	properties of lines and points in planes
6	properties of lines and points in planes
7	properties of lines and points in planes
8	properties of lines and points in planes
9	properties of lines and points in planes
10	properties of lines and points in planes
11	solving equations
12	solving equations
13	working with parallel lines
14	working with parallel lines
15	working with parallel lines
16	working with parallel lines
17	writing equations of lines
18	writing equations of lines
19	transforming polygons
20	transforming polygons
21	transforming polygons
22	transforming polygons
23	properties of triangles
24	properties of triangles
25	properties of triangles

Item Number	Skills
26	properties of triangles
27	properties of triangles
28	properties of triangles
29	properties of parallelograms
30	properties of parallelograms
31	properties of parallelograms
32	properties of parallelograms
33	properties of parallelograms
34	properties of parallelograms
35	similar triangles
36	similar triangles
37	similar triangles
38	solving right triangles
39	solving right triangles
40	properties of circles
41	properties of circles
42	properties of circles
43	properties of circles
44	finding volume of a solid
45	finding volume of a solid
46	finding arc length
47	finding sector area

Name _____   Date _____

Use the diagram.

1. Give two names for the plane.

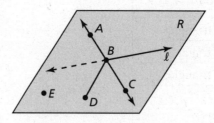

2. Name three collinear points.

3. Name three coplanar points.

4. Name three points.   5. Name one ray.

6. Name two lines.   7. Name one line segment.

Sketch the figure described.

8. $\overleftrightarrow{AB}$ and $\overrightarrow{AC}$

9. plane C and plane D intersecting at $\overleftrightarrow{XY}$

Find BD.

10.
B ———21——— C —7— D

11.
|——————— 73 ———————|
C 17 B   D

12. The endpoints of $\overline{QR}$ are $Q(1, 6)$ and $R(-7, 3)$. Find the coordinates of the midpoint M.

13. Find the distance between the two points $S(-5, -2)$ and $T(-3, 4)$.

14. Identify the segment bisector of $\overline{QR}$. Then find QR.

Q ——2x + 6—— M ——5x − 9—— R   (line ℓ)

15. The midpoint of $\overline{GH}$ is $M(4, -3)$. One endpoint is $G(-2, 2)$. Find the coordinates of endpoint H.

Answers

1. _____

_____

2. _____

_____

_____

3. _____

_____

4. _____

_____

_____

5. _____

6. _____

_____

7. _____

8. __See left.__

9. __See left.__

10. _____

11. _____

12. _____

13. _____

14. _____

15. _____

Name_____ Date_____

1. Find the length of $\overline{XY}$. Explain how you found your answer.

X — 6 — Z — 12 — Y

2. A map shows a section of Highway 18 that forms a straight line. A family plans to drive 440 miles on Highway 18 from Springfield to Columbia. They drive for 66 miles, and then decide they will stop halfway through their trip to rest for the night. How much farther do they need to drive before they stop for the night?

3. Point M is between points L and N on $\overline{LN}$. $LN = 6x$, $LM = 4x + 8$, and $MN = 27$. Use the information to solve for x, and then find LN.

L — 4x + 8 — M — 27 — N (with 6x spanning across the top)

Use the diagram.

4. Give another name for line S.

5. Name three points that are coplanar.

6. Name three points that are collinear.

7. Give another name for plane K

8. Plot the points in a coordinate plane. Then determine whether $\overline{AB}$ and $\overline{CD}$ are congruent: $A(\quad , \quad 1)$, $B(2, 1)$, $C(3, 2)$, $D(3, -2)$.

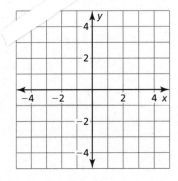

9. The endpoints of $\overline{CD}$ are $C(1, -6)$ and $D(7, 5)$. Find the coordinates of the midpoint M.

10. The midpoint of $\overline{RS}$ is $M(1, 2)$. One endpoint is $R(-6, 6)$. Find the coordinates of endpoint S.

Answers

1. _____

_____

_____

_____

2. _____

3. _____

4. _____

5. _____

_____

_____

6. _____

_____

_____

_____

7. _____

8. **See left.**

_____

9. _____

10. _____

Name _____ Date _____

Find the perimeter and area of the figure shown.

Answers

11.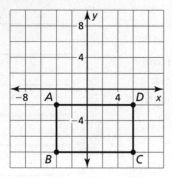

11. _____

   _____

12. _____

   _____

13. _____

   _____

Identify the segment bisector of $\overline{XY}$. Then find XY.

14. _____

12. 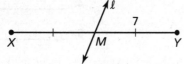   **13.**

   _____

15. _____

   _____

16. _____

$\overrightarrow{BD}$ **bisects ∠ABC. Use the diagram and the given angle measure to find the indicated angle measures.**

   _____

17. _____

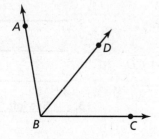

18. _____

19. _____

20. _____

14. $m\angle ABD = 57°$. Find $m\angle DBC$ and $m\angle ABC$.

15. $m\angle ABD = 70°$. Find $m\angle DBC$ and $m\angle ABC$.

16. $m\angle ABC = 110°$. Find $m\angle ABD$ and $m\angle DBC$.

Find the angle measure.

17. ∠B is a supplement of ∠A and $m\angle A = 65.2°$. Find $m\angle B$.

18. ∠B is a complement of ∠A and $m\angle A = 65.2°$. Find $m\angle B$.

19. ∠A is a supplement of ∠B and $m\angle B = (3x - 2)°$. Find $m\angle A$.

20. ∠A is a complement of ∠B and $m\angle B = (3x - 2)°$. Find $m\angle A$.

Name_____ Date _____

Test B

Use the figure.

Answers

1. Give another name for plane *R*.

2. Name a line that intersects the plane.

3. Name two rays.

4. Name a point on plane *R*.

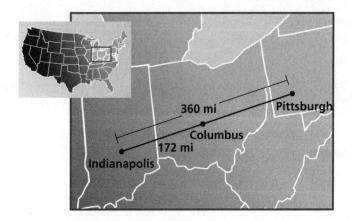

5. The cities shown on the map lie approximately in a straight line. Find the distance from Pittsburgh, Pennsylvania, to Columbus, Ohio.

1. _____

2. _____

3. _____

_____

4. _____

5. _____

6. _____

7. _____

8. _____

9. _____

10. _____

_____

The endpoints of $\overline{AB}$ are given. Find the coordinates of the midpoint C.

6. $A(-1, 9)$ and $B(-2, 5)$

7. $A(12, -5)$ and $B(-3, 2)$

The midpoint M and one endpoint of $\overline{CE}$ are given. Find the coordinates of the other endpoint.

8. $M\left(\frac{5}{2}, 1\right)$ and $E(-2, -3)$

9. $M(-1, 3)$ and $C(-4, 1)$

10. Identify the segment bisector of $\overline{RT}$. Then find RT

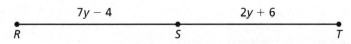

Chapter 1 **Test B** (continued)

11. a. Plot the points in the coordinate plane.

$A(1, 2)$, $B(1, 4)$, $C(6, 2)$,

$D(-3, 4)$, $E(-3, 6)$, $F(-8, 4)$

11. a. ___See left.___

b. Find the area of each triangle.

b. _____

c. Do the triangles have the same area? Explain.

c. _____

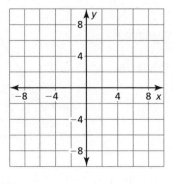

12. _____

13. _____

14. _____

Find the angle measure. Then classify the angle.

12. $m\angle MXN$

13. $m\angle NXP$

14. $m\angle OXQ$

15. _____

16. _____

17. _____

18. _____

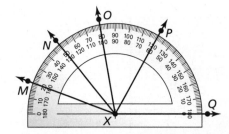

Use the diagram and the given angle measures to find the indicated angle measure.

15. $m\angle PQT = 51.5°$ and $m\angle TQR = 48°$.
Find $m\angle PQR$.

16. $m\angle PQR = 113°$ and $m\angle TQR = 30.25°$.
Find $m\angle PQT$.

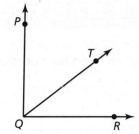

17. The tip of a pendulum is in a state of rest, hanging from point P. During an experiment, a physics student sets the pendulum in motion. The tip of the pendulum swings back and forth. The tip swings from point L to point N. During each swing, the tip passes through point M. Name all the angles in the diagram.

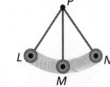

18. Your friend is making a pattern for quilt pieces. Her pattern is a right triangle with two acute angles that are complementary. The measure of one of the acute angles is to be $12°$ more than half the measure of the other acute angle. Find the measure of each angle of the triangle.

Name_____ Date _____

1. The folding breakfast menu consists of two flat, rectangular sections.

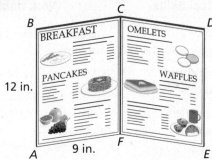

12 in.

9 in.

a. Name the intersection of plane *ABF* and plane *CDE*.

b. Name the intersection of plane *CDE* and $\overleftrightarrow{AF}$.

c. Name three different planes that contain point *C*.

d. Name a line that does not intersect plane *CDE*.

e. Classify ∠*BCD* when the menu is unfolded and laid flat on a table.

f. In the diagram, $\overline{AF} \cong \overline{FE}$ and $\overline{AB} \cong \overline{ED}$. Describe and justify two methods for finding the area covered by the unfolded menu laid flat on a table. Which method do you prefer and why?

2. The design of a flower pot charm for a charm bracelet is shown below.

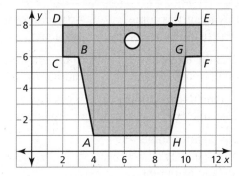

a. The charm is a polygon. Classify the polygon by the number of sides. State whether the polygon is *convex* or *concave*. Explain your reasoning.

b. Find the coordinates of the center of the hole, located at the midpoint of $\overline{CE}$.

c. Identify any congruent segments in the charm.

d. Given that $m\angle AHJ = 90°$ and $m\angle JHG \approx 11.3°$, find $m\angle AHG$.

e. In an alternate design, points *A* and *H* are changed to $A(5, 0)$ and $H(8, 0)$. Graph this design in a coordinate plane.

f. The perimeter of each charm is edged in gold. Which design uses less gold? Explain.

Name _____ Date _____

Score	Conceptual Understanding	Mathematical Skills	Work Habits
4	Shows complete understanding of: • naming points, lines, and planes and identifying their intersections • classifying angles and finding measures of angles and segments • finding area and perimeter	Correctly identifies all geometric features described Classifies the angle and polygon correctly Demonstrates understanding of finding area and perimeter Correctly applies all addition postulates and Distance and Midpoint Formulas	Answers all parts of both problems All answers are complete and correct. Work is very neat and well organized.
3	Shows nearly complete understanding of: • naming points, lines, and planes and identifying their intersections • classifying angles and finding measures of angles and segments • finding area and perimeter	Correctly identifies most geometric features described Classifies the angle and polygon correctly Demonstrates understanding of finding area or perimeter Correctly applies most addition postulates and Distance and Midpoint Formulas	Answers several parts of both problems Most answers are complete and correct. Work is neat and organized.
2	Shows some understanding of: • naming points, lines, and planes and identifying their intersections • classifying angles and finding measures of angles and segments • finding area and perimeter	Correctly identifies some geometric features described Classifies the angle or polygon correctly Shows some understanding of area or perimeter Correctly applies some addition postulates or Distance and Midpoint Formulas	Answers some parts of both problems Many answers are incomplete and incorrect. Work is not very neat or organized.
1	Shows little understanding of: • naming points, lines, and planes and identifying their intersections • classifying angles and finding measures of angles and segments • finding area and perimeter	Misidentifies many geometric features Classifies the angle or polygon correctly Demonstrates poor understanding of area or perimeter Fails to find most distances and measures correctly	Provides very few answers for either problem Almost none of the answers are correct. Work is sloppy and disorganized.

Name_____ Date _____

Comfortable Horse Stalls

Instructional Overview	
Launch Question	The plan for a new barn includes standard, rectangular horse stalls. The architect is sure that this will provide the most comfort for your horse because it is the greatest area for the stall. Is that correct? How can you investigate to find out?
Summary	Students investigate the area of a rectangle, given a fixed perimeter, in three ways: numerically in a table, algebraically in an equation, and graphically with a graphing calculator. They learn that the maximum area for a fixed perimeter occurs when the side lengths are equal (when the rectangle is a square).
Teacher Notes	For Exercise 1, students should sketch a rectangle for each table entry to see the dimensions of the stall changing.
	For Exercise 2, students should be familiar with using the *maximum* feature of a graphing calculator. If they struggle to change their viewing window correctly, direct them to the "area" column of their completed table in Exercise 1, and ask them to explain the domain and range of the area function.
	Emphasize the difference in units between the perimeter (linear) and area (squared).
Supplies	Calculators
Mathematical Discourse	How can mathematics help you as a consumer or customer?
Writing/Discussion Prompts	1. What is the difference between perimeter and area?
	2. What are other examples of applications in which you might want the largest area for a fixed perimeter?

Curriculum Content	
Content Objectives	• Use geometric shapes, their measures, and their properties to solve a design problem with given constraints.
	• Use tables, equations, and graphs to represent functions that model the relationships between two quantities.
	• Create equations in two variables to represent the relationships between two quantities and to represent constraints placed on the quantities.
	• Rewrite equations to focus on a quantity of interest.
Mathematical Practices	• Model the area of rectangles by writing equations.
	• Use appropriate tools, such as tables, functions, and graphing calculators.

Chapter 1 Performance Task (continued)

Comfortable Horse Stalls

Rubric

Comfortable Horse Stalls	Points	
1. Correct answers in form of (length, width, perimeter, area): (5, 17, 44, 85), (6, 16, 44, 96), (7, 15, 44, 105), (8, 14, 44, 112), (9, 13, 44, 117), (10, 12, 44, 120), (11, 11, 44, 121), (12, 10, 44, 120); no; The largest area derives from the 11-foot by 11-foot square.	**5** **3** **1**	Table is correctly completed and sketches of possible stalls are included Table is correct but some stalls are not correctly drawn Table is incorrect
2. a. $A = \ell \bullet w$ b. $2\ell + 2w = 44$ c. $\ell = 22 - w$ d. $A(w) = (22 - w) \bullet w = 22w - w^2$ e. window must expand to at least x-max of 15 and y-max of 125, graph represents area in terms of width f. max area is 121 ft^2 when width is 11 ft, meaning length is also 11 ft; The maximum area of 121 ft^2 should agree with the student's table.	**6**	Equations and explanations are correct. (1 point for each section)
3. The maximum area comes with the shape of a square, when the sides are of equal length. *Sample answer:* You can fit more horses in one barn with rectangular stalls because horses are not square; more convenient for daily maintenance	**3** **2** **1**	Answer is correct, and explanation is thorough Answer is correct but explanation is incorrect or not given Neither answer nor explanation is correct
Mathematics Practice: Use appropriate tools strategically. Students should be able to explain their problem-solving process using all three methods of investigation.	**2**	Demonstration of practice; Partial credit can be awarded
Total Points	**16 points**	

Name_____ Date _____

Comfortable Horse Stalls

The plan for a new barn includes standard, rectangular horse stalls. The architect is sure that this will provide the most comfort for your horse because it is the greatest area for the stall. Is that correct? How can you investigate to find out?

The budget for your new barn allows for a horse stall with a total perimeter of 44 feet. The stall in the current plans is 10-foot by 12-foot, an industry standard.

1. a. Explore the options for the dimensions of the stall by completing the table. Then sketch each stall on the coordinate plane as shown for the 10-foot by 12-foot stall.

Length (in feet)	Width (in feet)	Perimeter	Area
5			
6			
7			
8			
9			
10	12	44	
11			
12			

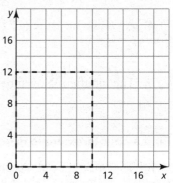

b. From your table, does a 10-foot by 12-foot stall provide the most area? If not, which size stall does?

2. Now investigate this problem algebraically and graphically.

a. Write an equation for A, the area of the stall, in terms of length ℓ and width w.

b. Write an equation for the perimeter of the stall in terms of length ℓ and width w, given that the perimeter is 44 feet.

c. Solve the perimeter equation for length ℓ.

d. Substitute the expression for length found in part (b) into your equation for area found in part (a). Write your new equation $A(w)$.

e. Use a graphing calculator to graph the area function $A(w)$ changing the viewing window until you see the maximum of the function. Explain what the function represents in terms of the domain and range.

f. Using the *maximum* feature on your calculator, what is the maximum area? What dimensions correspond to this area? Does this agree with your table?

3. What rectangular shape has the largest area for a fixed perimeter? Why might barn owners choose to build standard 10-foot by 12-foot barn stalls instead of stalls in this shape?

Name _____ Date _____

Describe the pattern. Then write or draw the next two numbers or figures.

Answers

1. 1, 4, 9, 16, 25, …

2. ☐ ⬡ ⯃

1. _____

   _____

2. _____

   _____

Rewrite the conditional statement in if-then form. Then write the converse, inverse, and contrapositive of the conditional statement. Decide whether each statement is true or false.

3. It is noon when the clock strikes 12.

3. __See left.__

4. __See left.__

5. __See left.__

4. An angle measure of 87° is an acute angle.

5. The month of November is after December.

6. _____

7. _____

Find a counterexample to show that the conjecture is false.

8. __See left.__

6. The difference of a positive number and a negative number is always positive.

9. __See left.__

10. _____

7. If a triangle measures 180°, each angle is 60°.

11. _____

Use inductive reasoning to make a conjecture about the given quantity. Then use deductive reasoning to show that the conjecture is true.

12. _____

8. the quotient of two negative numbers

13. _____

14. _____

9. the sum of the absolute values of any two numbers

Use the diagram to determine whether you can assume the statement.

10. Plane *S* is perpendicular to plane *T*.

11. Points *E*, *B*, and *D* are collinear.

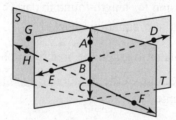

12. ∠*ABE* is a right angle.

13. Line $\overleftrightarrow{DE}$ lies in plane *T*.

14. $\overleftrightarrow{AC}$ and $\overleftrightarrow{DE}$ intersect.

Name_____ Date _____

Use the diagram to determine whether the statement is true or false.

Answers

1. Points *D*, *G*, and *F* are collinear.

2. ∠*ABH* is a right angle.

3. ∠*ABH* and ∠*CBH* are complementary.

4. $\overleftrightarrow{IH}$ is perpendicular to line *m*.

5. ∠*DEH* and ∠*FEH* are supplementary.

6. $\overline{CB}$ is perpendicular to line ℓ.

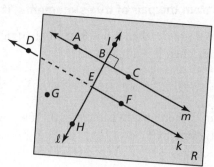

1. _____

2. _____

3. _____

4. _____

5. _____

6. _____

7. _____

Determine whether the conditional statement is true. If false, give a counterexample.

7. If two planes intersect, then they intersect in exactly one point.

8. If two lines intersect, then they form four angles.

Write the converse and inverse of the statement.

9. If it is Sunday, then it is the weekend.

10. If *m*∠*A* = 95°, then ∠*A* is obtuse.

11. If an animal is a bird, then it has two eyes.

8. _____

_____

9. ___See left.___

10. ___See left.___

11. ___See left.___

12. _____

13. _____

14. _____

_____

Decide whether inductive reasoning or deductive reasoning is used to reach the conclusion.

12. Gas prices have gone up every day this week. The price of gas will go up tomorrow.

13. What goes up must come down. The ball went up. It will come down.

15. _____

_____

Use the Law of Detachment to determine what you can conclude from the given information, if possible.

14. If three points lie on the same line, they are collinear. Points *A*, *B*, and *C* lie on line ℓ.

15. If it is hailing, then you are not going outdoors. It is hailing.

Chapter 2 **Test A** (continued)

Use the Law of Syllogism to draw a conclusion to write a new conditional statement that follows from the pair of true statements, if possible.

16. If a quadrilateral is a square, then it has four right angles. If a quadrilateral has four right angles, then it is a rectangle.

17. If a number ends in 0, then it is divisible by 10. If a number is divisible by 10, then it is divisible by 5.

Solve the equation. Justify each step.

18. $\dfrac{x + 3}{-2} = 8$

19. $5x - 3 = 4(x - 2)$

20. You and your brother borrowed money to buy a car from a local bank at an annual simple interest rate of 5%. The amount of interest I is represented by the equation $I = Prt$ where P is the principal amount, r is the rate (in decimal form), and t is the time (in years). Solve the formula for P, then find the principal amount when the interest is $7500 and the time is 6 years. Be sure to justify each step.

Identify the property that justifies the statement.

21. $KL = PR$, so $PR = KL$

22. $614 = 614$

23. If $a = b$ and $b = c$, then $a = c$.

Write a proof using any format.

24. **Given** $\angle 1$ and $\angle 2$ are supplementary, $m\angle 1 = 135°$

Prove $m\angle 2 = 45°$

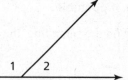

Answers

16. ____See left.____

17. ____See left.____

18. _____

    ____See left.____

19. _____

    ____See left.____

20. _____

    _____

    ____See left.____

21. _____

22. _____

23. _____

24. ____See left.____

Chapter 2 Test B

Write the if-then form of the conditional statement.

Answers

1. It is time for dinner if it is 6 P.M.

1. _____

2. The measure of a right angle is 90°.

_____

Write the converse of the conditional statement. If the converse is false, provide a counterexample.

2. _____

3. If two angles are not adjacent, then they are vertical angles.

_____

4. If x is odd, then $3x$ is odd.

3. _____

Write the inverse of the conditional statement.

_____

5. If an angle measures 30°, then it is acute.

4. _____

6. If two angles are supplementary, then their sum is 180°.

_____

Write the contrapositive of the conditional statement.

5. _____

7. If an animal is a panther, then it lives in the forest.

_____

8. If two angles have the same measure, then they are congruent.

6. _____

Use the diagram to determine whether the statement is true or false.

_____

9. Points A, B, and L are coplanar.

7. _____

10. $\overleftrightarrow{JL}$ lies on plane K.

_____

11. $\overleftrightarrow{DF}$ intersects $\overleftrightarrow{AC}$.

8. _____

12. Points D, F, and E are collinear.

_____

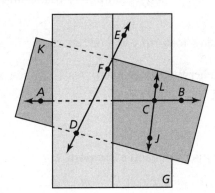

9. _____

10. _____

11. _____

Solve the equation. Justify each step.

12. _____

13. $-8x + 7 = -33$

13. _____

____See left.____

14. $9x - 5 = 3x + 7$

14. _____

____See left.____

15. $2(4x - 3) - 8 = 4 + 2x$

15. _____

____See left.____

Chapter 2 Test B (continued)

16. A gardener has 26 feet of fencing for a garden. To find the width of the rectangular garden, the gardener uses the formula $P = 2\ell + 2w$, where P is the perimeter, ℓ is the length, and w is the width of the rectangle. The gardener wants to fence a garden that is 8 feet long and plans on using all of the available fencing. How wide is the garden? Solve the equation for w, and justify each step.

17. Use the diagram to find the value of x and the measure of each angle. Write a justification for each step.

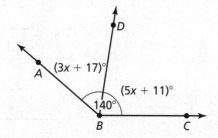

Decide whether inductive reasoning or deductive reasoning is used to reach the conclusion.

18. Because today is Friday, tomorrow will be Saturday.

19. Sandy earned A's on her first six geometry tests, so she concludes that she will always earn A's on geometry tests.

20. If $5x = 25$, then $x = 5$.

Identify the property that justifies each statement.

21. If $m\angle ABC = m\angle DEF$, then $m\angle DEF = m\angle ABC$.

22. If $AB = CD$ and $CD = EF$, then $AB = EF$.

23. $x = y$; If $y = 9$, then $x = 9$.

24. $W = W$

Write a proof using any format.

25. Given $m\angle 1 + m\angle 2 = 90°$,
$\qquad\quad m\angle 3 + m\angle 4 = 90°$

Prove $m\angle 1 = m\angle 4$

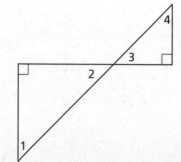

Answers

16. _____

_____See left._____

17. _____

_____See left._____

18. _____

19. _____

20. _____

21. _____

22. _____

23. _____

24. _____

25. _____See left._____

Name_____ Date_____

1. You and your friend are comparing the locations of the stores at a mall in your city. Your friend describes the relative locations of some of the mall stores in the following way.

   The clothing store *C* is located along Hallway 1. The food court *F* is due east of the clothing store along Hallway 1. The music store *M* is northeast of the food court so that ∠*CFM* is obtuse. The food court and music store are along Hallway 2. The bookstore *B* is southeast of the food court so that ∠*MFB* is acute. The food court and bookstore are along Hallway 3. The shoe store *S* is due east of the food court on Hallway 1.

   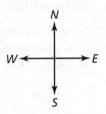

   a. Use your friend's description to draw a diagram showing the relative locations of the stores.

   b. Where do the hallways intersect?

   c. You and your friend go to the clothing store and see two signs. One sign reads "All summer clothes are on sale." Another sign reads "The sale price is 30% off the original price." Write each sign's statement in if-then form.

   d. Use deductive reasoning to write a new conditional statement from the statements in part (c).

   e. Write the converse, the inverse, and the contrapositive of the statement you wrote in part (d).

   f. Is ∠*SFB* acute or obtuse? Explain your reasoning.

2. Write a proof using any format.

   Given ∠3 ≅ ∠2

   Prove ∠1 and ∠3 are supplementary.

   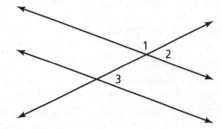

Name _____ Date _____

Alternative Assessment Rubric

Score	Conceptual Understanding	Mathematical Skills	Work Habits
4	Shows complete understanding of: • if-then form, deductive reasoning, converse, inverse, and contrapositive • proving a statement using given information and a logical progression of statements and reasons	Correctly answers all parts in Question 1 Writes a complete and logical proof in Question 2	Answers all parts of both questions The answers are explained thoroughly with mathematical terminology. Work is very neat and well organized.
3	Shows nearly complete understanding of: • if-then form, deductive reasoning, converse, inverse, and contrapositive • proving a statement using given information and a logical progression of statements and reasons	Correctly answers most parts in Question 1 Writes a nearly complete and logical proof in Question 2	Answers most parts of both questions The answers are explained with mathematical terminology. Work is neat and organized.
2	Shows some understanding of: • if-then form, deductive reasoning, converse, inverse, and contrapositive • proving a statement using given information and a logical progression of statements and reasons	Correctly answers some parts in Question 1 Writes an incomplete or illogical proof in Question 2	Answers some parts of both questions The answers are poorly or incorrectly explained. Work is not very neat or organized.
1	Shows little understanding of: • if-then form, deductive reasoning, converse, inverse, and contrapositive • proving a statement using given information and a logical progression of statements and reasons	Does not answer or has all incorrect answers to the parts in Question 1 Does not answer or does not complete the proof in Question 2	Attempts few parts of either question No explanation is included with the answers. Work is sloppy and disorganized.

Name_____ Date _____

Performance Task

Induction and the Next Dimension

Instructional Overview	
Launch Question	Before you took geometry, you could find the midpoint of a line segment on a number line, a one-dimensional system. In Chapter 1, you learned how to find the midpoint of a line segment on a coordinate plane, a two-dimensional system. How would you find the midpoint of a line segment in a three-dimensional system?
Summary	One goal of this task is to build students' confidence in their own mathematical knowledge and intuition. Students will use knowledge about number lines and the coordinate plane, one- and two-dimensional systems respectively, to extend formulas and find the midpoint of a line segment in a three-dimensional space.
Teacher Notes	Extending the flat coordinate plane into the third dimension of space will be new to students. They may not initially know what to call the vertical axis and may hesitate to follow the alphabetical pattern already established for the x- and y-axes. Encourage them to trust alphabetical order when guessing the name of the z-axis. In three dimensions, we basically lay the x-y plane down flat, with the x-axis coming out of the page, the y-axis going horizontally across the page, and the z-axis going vertically up the page. Encourage students to look at the floor corner of the room to see the three-dimensional space.
Supplies	Task handout
Mathematical Discourse	What do you think of when you hear "3-D"? What is the difference between this and "1-D"? "2-D"?
Writing/Discussion Prompts	1. Why is the progression in inductive reasoning based on integers?

Chapter 2 Performance Task (continued)

Induction and the Next Dimension

Curriculum Content	
Content Objectives	• Extend the concept of the midpoint of a line segment in the coordinate plane to the midpoint of a line segment in the coordinate space. • Interpret the expressions for the midpoints of line segments in one-, two-, and three-dimensions.
Mathematical Practices	• Reason abstractly to generalize the patterns of one- and two-dimensions and then write an expression for the midpoint of a line segment in three-dimensions. • Look for and express repeated reasoning to write the expression for the z-coordinate of the midpoint of a line segment in three-dimensions.

Rubric

Induction and the Next Dimension	Points	
1. $x_1 = -2$; $x_2 = 4$; $M = 1$	2	Midpoint is correctly calculated and labeled on number line.
	1	Midpoint is incorrect but this value is correctly labeled.
	0	Neither is correct.
2. $P_1(1, 3)$; $P_2(5, -1)$; $M(3, 1)$ $x_1\,y_1 \ x_2\ y_2$	2	Midpoint is correctly calculated and labeled on number line.
	1	Midpoint is incorrect but this value is correctly labeled.
	0	Neither is correct.
3. three; three; z; triples; $P_1(1, 0, 5)$; $P_2(3, 2, 1)$; triple; $\dfrac{z_1 + z_2}{2}$	5	All blanks are correct.
	3	Most blanks are correct.
	1	Few blanks are correct.
$M(2, 1, 3)$	5	Calculation is correct for all coordinates.
	3	Two coordinates are correct.
	1	One coordinate is correct.
Mathematics Practice: Express regularity in repeated reasoning. Students should be able to generalize the calculation in the third coordinate of the Midpoint Formula in a three-dimensional space.	2	For demonstration of practice; Partial credit can be awarded.
Total Points	**16 points**	

Name_____ Date_____

Induction and the Next Dimension

Before you took geometry, you could find the midpoint of a line segment on a number line, a one-dimensional system. In Chapter 1, you learned how to find the midpoint of a line segment on a coordinate plane, a two-dimensional system. How would you find the midpoint of a line segment in a three-dimensional system?

1. For $n = 1$, we have a one-dimensional system. We represent that system graphically with one coordinate axis and one variable, x. We represent positions on that line with a single number. For this example:

   $x_1 = $ _____ $x_2 = $ _____

   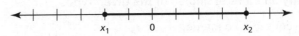

   To find the midpoint, use the formula

   $$M\left(\frac{x_1 + x_2}{2}\right).$$

   Find and label the midpoint of this one-dimensional segment: M_____

2. For $n = 2$, we have a two-dimensional system. We represent that system graphically by a coordinate plane made from two coordinate axes and points consisting of two variables, x and y. We represent positions on that plane with ordered pairs. For this example:

   $P_1(\underline{}, \underline{})$ $P_2(\underline{}, \underline{})$
       x_1 y_1 x_2 y_2

   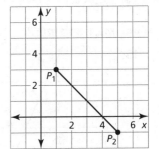

   To find the midpoint, which is also an ordered pair, use the formula

   $$M\left(\frac{x_1 + x_2}{2}, \frac{y_1 + y_2}{2}\right).$$

   Find and label the midpoint of this two-dimensional segment: M_____

3. Use induction to analyze the next dimension. For $n = 3$, we have a _____-dimensional system. We represent that system graphically with a coordinate space and points consisting of _____ variables, x, y, and _____. We represent positions on that line with ordered _____. For this example:

   $P_1(\underline{}, \underline{}, \underline{})$ $P_2 = (\underline{}, \underline{}, \underline{})$
       x_1 y_1 ___ x_2 y_2 ___

   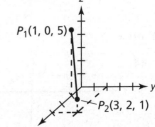

   To find the midpoint, which is also an ordered _____, use the formula

   $$M\left(\frac{x_1 + x_2}{2}, \frac{y_1 + y_2}{2}, \underline{}\right).$$

   Find and label the midpoint of this _____-dimensional segment: M_____

Name_____ Date _____

Think of each segment in the diagram as part of a line. Which line(s) or plane(s) contain point *R* and appear to fit the description?

Answers

1. line(s) parallel to $\overrightarrow{SP}$

2. line(s) perpendicular to $\overrightarrow{SP}$

3. line(s) skew to $\overrightarrow{SP}$

4. plane(s) parallel to plane *KLM*

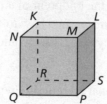

1. _____

2. _____

3. _____

4. _____

5. _____

_____

Identify all pairs of angles of the given type.

5. consecutive interior

6. alternate interior

7. corresponding

8. alternate exterior

9. vertical

6. _____

_____

7. _____

_____

_____

8. _____

Find *m∠1* and *m∠2*.

10.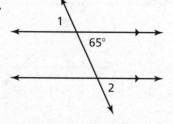

11.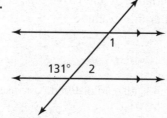

_____

9. _____

_____

_____

10. _____

11. _____

Decide whether there is enough information to prove that *j* is parallel to *k*. If so, state the theorem you would use.

12.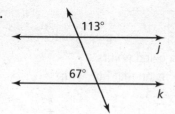

13.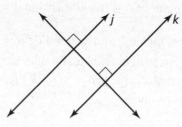

12. _____

_____

13. _____

_____

Find *x*.

14.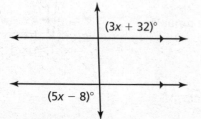

15.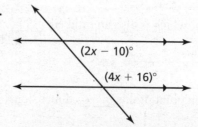

14. _____

15. _____

Chapter 3 Test A

Identify an example on the box of the description.

Answers

1. a pair of skew lines

2. a pair of perpendicular lines

3. a pair of parallel lines

4. a pair of intersecting planes and where they intersect

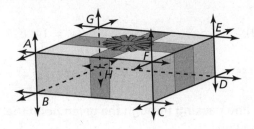

1. _____

2. _____

3. _____

4. _____

5. _____

Find the values of x and y. State which theorem(s) you used.

5.

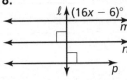

6.

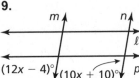

7.

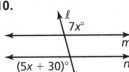

6. _____

_____

7. _____

Find the value of x that makes m ∥ n.

8.

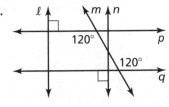

9.

10.

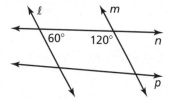

8. _____

9. _____

10. _____

11. _____

Determine which lines, if any, must be parallel. Explain your reasoning.

11.

12.

12. _____

_____

_____

Complete the sentence.

13. The slopes of perpendicular lines are _____.

14. Parallel lines have the _____ slope.

15. The shortest distance from any point to a line is a _____.

13. _____

14. _____

15. _____

Chapter 3 **Test A** (continued)

Write the equation of the line passing through the given point that is **parallel** to the given line.

16. $y = \frac{2}{3}x - 2;\ (-3, 4)$

17. $-2x + 7y = 14;\ (-7, -3)$

18. $3x - 4y = 16;\ (8, -5)$

19. $4x + y = 7;\ (2, 4)$

Write the equation of the line passing through the given point that is **perpendicular** to the given line.

20. $y = \frac{2}{3}x - 2;\ (-2, 4)$

21. $-2x + 7y = 14;\ (-3, -7)$

22. $3x - 8y = 16;\ (-3, 1)$

23. $4x + y = 7;\ (4, 2)$

Determine which lines, if any, are *parallel* or *perpendicular*.

24. Line a: $y = 5x - 6$

Line b: $x + 5y = 5$

25. Line a: $2x + y = 10$

Line b: $-6x - 3y = 3$

Line c: $x - 2y = 8$

Answers

16. _____

17. _____

18. _____

19. _____

20. _____

21. _____

22. _____

23. _____

24. _____

_____

25. _____

_____

36 **Geometry**
Assessment Book

Name_____ Date_____

Find the values of *x* and *y*. State which theorem(s) you used.

Answers

1.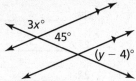

2.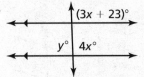

3.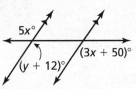

1. _____

_____

2. _____

4. When two parallel lines are cut by a transversal, name the angles that are congruent.

5. When two parallel lines are cut by a transversal, name the angles that are supplementary.

3. _____

_____

4. _____

Find the value of *x* that makes line *m* ∥ *n*.

6.

7.

8.

5. _____

_____

Write the equation of the line that passes through the given point and is parallel to the given line.

9. $(-3, -4)$; $y = \frac{1}{2}x - 8$

10. $(3, 6)$; $2x - 6y = 12$

6. _____

7. _____

Write the equation of the line that passes through the given point and is perpendicular to the given line.

11. $(4, -2)$; $y = -2x - 8$

12. $(2, 3)$; $4x - 6y = 18$

8. _____

9. _____

10. _____

Determine if the lines are *parallel*, *perpendicular*, or *neither*.

13. $y = 3x - 5$; $y = -3x + 1$

14. $2x + 3y = 15$; $4x + 6y = -48$

15. $6x - 12y = -24$; $3y = 2x + 18$

16. $4x + 2y = 10$; $y = \frac{1}{2}x + 15$

11. _____

12. _____

13. _____

Use the coordinate plane diagram.

17. Find the equation of the line from your friend's house to her school.

18. Find the equation of the line from the school to the library.

19. What is the distance from your friend's house to the school?

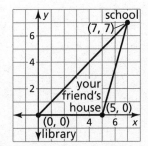

14. _____

15. _____

16. _____

17. _____

18. _____

19. _____

Chapter 3 **Test B** (continued)

Identify an example on the box of the description. Explain your reasoning.

20. a pair of skew lines

21. a pair of perpendicular lines

22. a pair of parallel lines

23. a pair of corresponding angles

Answers

20. _____

21. _____

22. _____

23. _____

24. See left.

25. See left.

Write a two-column proof.

24. **Given** $\ell \parallel m$ and $\angle 1 \cong \angle 7$

Prove $a \parallel b$

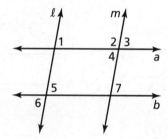

25. **Given** $a \parallel b$ and $\angle 5$ is supplementary to $\angle 2$.

Prove $\ell \parallel m$

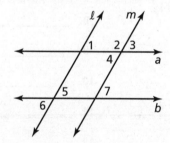

Chapter 3 Alternative Assessment

1. The figure shows part of a lattice tower for a cell site such that $p \parallel q$.

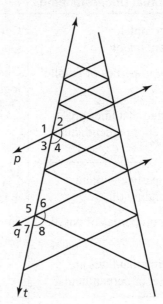

   a. Identify each pair of corresponding angles, alternate interior angles, alternate exterior angles, and consecutive interior angles formed by lines p, q, and t.

   b. Identify all the congruent angles formed by lines p, q, and t.

   c. Find the value of x that makes $p \parallel q$ when $m\angle 2 = 44°$ and $m\angle 5 = 2x°$.

   d. Find the value of x that makes $p \parallel q$ when $m\angle 4 = 110°$ and $m\angle 8 = 4x°$.

   e. A design specification requires that $3 \bullet m\angle 3 \le m\angle 1 \le 150°$. Do either of the situations described in parts (c) and (d) meet this specification? Explain your reasoning.

2. In the figure, $m \parallel n$ and $\ell \perp m$.

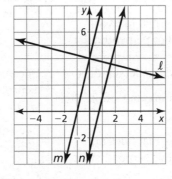

   a. Explain how to show that two lines are parallel using angles.

   b. Use your explanation in part (a) to show that $m \parallel n$.

   c. Explain how to show that two lines are parallel using slopes.

   d. Use your explanation in part (c) to show that $m \parallel n$.

   e. Explain how to show that two lines are perpendicular using angles.

   f. Use your explanation in part (e) to show that $\ell \perp m$.

   g. Explain how to show that two lines are perpendicular using slopes.

   h. Use your explanation in part (g) to show that $\ell \perp m$.

Chapter 3 Alternative Assessment Rubric

Score	Conceptual Understanding	Mathematical Skills	Work Habits
4	Shows complete understanding of: • using properties of parallel lines • showing that lines are parallel or perpendicular	Correctly answers all parts in Question 1 Gives correct, clear, and logical answers to all parts of Question 2	Answers all parts of both questions The answers are explained thoroughly with mathematical terminology. Work is very neat and well organized.
3	Shows nearly complete understanding of: • using properties of parallel lines • showing that lines are parallel or perpendicular	Correctly answers most parts in Question 1 Gives correct, clear, and logical answers to most parts of Question 2	Answers most parts of both questions The answers are explained with mathematical terminology. Work is neat and organized.
2	Shows some understanding of: • using properties of parallel lines • showing that lines are parallel or perpendicular	Correctly answers some parts in Question 1 Gives correct, clear, and logical answers to some parts of Question 2	Answers some parts of both questions. The answers are poorly or incorrectly explained. Work is not very neat or organized.
1	Shows little understanding of: • using properties of parallel lines • showing that lines are parallel or perpendicular	Does not answer or has all incorrect answers to the parts in Question 1 Does not answer or gives all incorrect, unclear, and illogical answers in Question 2	Attempts few parts of any question No explanation is included with the answers. Work is sloppy and disorganized.

Name_____ Date_____

 Performance Task

Navajo Rugs

Instructional Overview	
Launch Question	Navajo rugs use mathematical properties to enhance their beauty. How can you describe these creative works of art with geometry? What properties of lines can you see and use to describe the patterns?
Summary	Students will superimpose a coordinate system on a Navajo rug. They will then select pairs of lines to describe the artwork, describe the angle relationships, and find some of the equations.
Teacher Notes	Explore online sites for Navajo rugs. One possible site is *http://navajorug.com*. Students can print their choice, or you could select and print some of the choices before the performance task day. If possible, make transparencies of the coordinate grid so that students can use it to find the equations. The pictures of the rugs should have lines that are parallel and, if possible, perpendicular. If there is not a perpendicular relationship, instruct the students to find a line in the rug and draw a perpendicular line to use.
Supplies	Straightedges, black markers, transparencies with coordinate grids
Mathematical Discourse	Why do you think Navajo people made rugs with patterns that included different types of lines?
Writing/Discussion Prompts	1. What do you like about the pattern in the rug you selected? 2. What types of lines appeared the most in your pattern? 3. Do you think that any of the angle relationships of parallel lines helped when creating the rugs? Why?

Curriculum Content	
Content Objectives	• Identify parallel and transversal lines and the relationships of the pairs of angles formed by the lines. • Write equations of lines from graphs in the coordinate plane and use the slopes to determine whether the lines are parallel or perpendicular.
Mathematical Practices	• Use a coordinate plane to model the design in a rug. • Use tools, such as a coordinate plane and a straightedge, to discover and analyze patterns in the design of a rug.

Chapter 3 Performance Task (continued)

Rubric

Navajo Rugs	Points	
Part 1: *Sample answer:* The slopes of the perpendicular lines are 1 and −1.	**8** **6** **4** **2** **1**	All lines drawn and angles labeled, shape selected One minor error in labeling Either the perpendicular lines or the parallel lines are correct. Lines drawn and many of the angles are labeled incorrectly Lines drawn or shape selected
Part 2: *Sample answer:* The student should have written two equations of parallel lines drawn in Part 1. These equations will vary depending on the lines drawn by the student; Explanations of methods will vary; The slopes should be the same; The lines should be parallel; Lines with the same slope are parallel.	**4** **1** **1** **1**	Total possible points for each correct equation for explanation of method for explanation of same slope for parallel lines
Sample answer: The student should have written two equations of perpendicular lines drawn in Part 1. These equations will vary depending on the lines drawn by the student; The slopes should be negative reciprocals; The lines should be perpendicular; Lines with slopes that are negative reciprocals of each other are perpendicular.	**5** **1** **1** **1**	Total possible points for each correct equation for each correct slope for explanation of negative reciprocals for perpendicular lines
Part 3: *Sample answer:* The student should have used three concepts learned in the chapter (such as parallel lines, perpendicular lines, and transversals) to describe the rug. The student should have identified a shape in the rug and described it using terms learned in the chapter.	**4** **1** **1**	Total possible points for each concept used to describe the rug for the additional shape selected and described
Mathematics Practice: Use appropriate tools strategically. Each student will use a straightedge and a coordinate plane to develop the equations.	**2**	The coordinate plane and coordinates of the points are used correctly. Partial credit can be awarded.
Total Points	**23 points**	

Name_____ Date _____

Navajo Rugs

Navajo rugs use mathematical properties to enhance their beauty. How can you describe these creative works of art with geometry? What properties of lines can you see and use to describe the patterns?

Use the Internet or another source as directed by your teacher to find an image of a Navajo rug that contains parallel and perpendicular lines.

Part 1: Print the image and draw the *x*- and *y*-axes on the rug.

1. Identify at least one set of parallel lines and a transversal line. Draw the lines on the graph.

    a. Label one set of corresponding angles $\angle 1$ and $\angle 2$.

    b. Label an alternate interior angle to one of the angles as $\angle 3$.

    c. Label a pair of alternate exterior angles $\angle 4$ and $\angle 5$.

2. Find a pair of angles that look like they would be perpendicular. Draw the lines on the rug graph.

    a. Label a set of vertical angles with $\angle 6$ and $\angle 7$.

    b. Estimate the slopes of your two lines.

3. Select any set of lines or shape that you see in the rug pattern. Draw in the shape on the graph.

Part 2: Creating equations

4. Find the equations of the two parallel lines you selected. Explain the method you used to find the equations. What is the slope of your two lines? Are they really parallel? How do you know?

5. Find the equations of the two lines you selected that look perpendicular. What are their slopes? Are they perpendicular? How do you know? If they are not, what is the slope for a line that would be perpendicular to one of your lines?

Part 3: Summary

6. Use at least 3 of the concepts you learned in this chapter to describe your rug and an additional shape.

Performance Task (continued)

Navajo Rugs

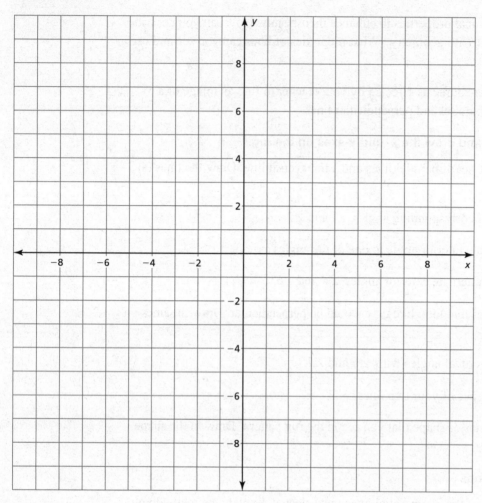

Name_____ Date _____

Performance Task (continued)

Teacher Notes:

Geometry **45**
Assessment Book

Chapters 1–3 **Cumulative Test**

1. Use the diagram to determine which segments, if any, are congruent. List all congruent segments.

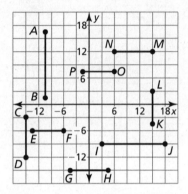

2. Which of the following terms are *undefined terms*?

| plane | segment | line | point | ray |

3. A line segment has a midpoint of $\left(2, \frac{3}{2}\right)$ and a length of 15 units. Which choice shows the correct endpoints of the line segment?

   A. $(0, 0)$ and $(4, 3)$

   B. $(-5, -2)$ and $(7, 7)$

   C. $(-4, -3)$ and $(8, 6)$

   D. $(-2, 1)$ and $(6, 2)$

4. Find the perimeter and area of the figure shown.

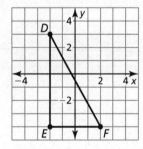

Chapters 1–3 **Cumulative Test** (continued)

5. Plot the points $A(-5, 4)$, $B(5, 4)$, $C(5, -1)$, and $D(-5, -1)$ in a coordinate plane. What type of polygon do the points form? Your friend claims that you could use this figure to represent a swimming pool with an area of 1250 square meters and a perimeter of 150 meters. Is your friend correct? Explain.

6. Use the steps in the construction to explain how you know that $\overline{CD}$ has the same length as $\overline{AB}$.

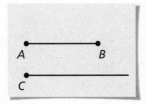 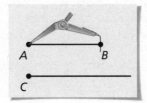 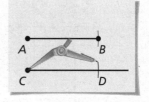

7. Four roads come to an intersection point that the people in your town call "Confusion Corner," as shown in the figure.

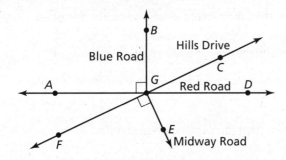

   a. Identify all vertical angles.

   b. Identify all right angles.

   c. Identify all linear pairs.

Chapters 1–3 **Cumulative Test** (continued)

8. Use the diagram to write an example of each postulate.

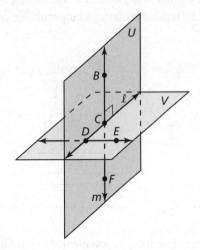

a. **Postulate 2.1** Through any two points, there exists exactly one line.

b. **Postulate 2.3** If two lines intersect, then their intersection is exactly one point.

c. **Postulate 2.4** Through any three collinear points, there exists exactly one plane.

d. **Postulate 2.6** If two points lie in a plane, then the line containing them lies in the plane.

e. **Postulate 2.7** If two planes intersect, then their intersection is a line.

9. Classify each related conditional statement based on the conditional statement "If Bobby sells five more magazines, then he will be the top seller."

a. If Bobby was the top seller, then he sold five more magazines.

b. If Bobby is not the top seller, then he did not sell five more magazines.

c. Bobby is the top seller if and only if he sells five more magazines.

d. If Bobby does not sell five more magazines, then he will not be the top seller.

Chapters 1–3 **Cumulative Test** (continued)

10. Enter the reasons in the correct positions to complete the two-column proof.

    Given $\overline{AB} \cong \overline{FE}, \overline{AC} \cong \overline{FD}$

    Prove $\overline{BC} \cong \overline{ED}$

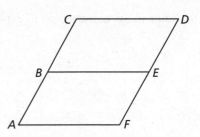

STATEMENTS	REASONS
1. $\overline{AB} \cong \overline{FE}$	1. Given
2. $AB = FE$	2.
3. $\overline{AC} \cong \overline{FD}$	3. Given
4. $AC = FD$	4.
5. $AB + BC = AC$	5.
6. $FE + BC = FD$	6.
7. $BC = FD - FE$	7.
8. $FE + ED = FD$	8.
9. $ED = FD - FE$	9.
10. $BC = ED$	10.
11. $\overline{BC} \cong \overline{ED}$	11.

Subtraction Property of Equality

Definition of congruent segments

Substitution Property of Equality

Segment Addition Postulate

11. Find the distance between each pair of points. Then order each line segment from shortest to longest.

    a. $A(-5, 2), B(-2, 5)$

    b. $C(-3, 7), D(3, 7)$

    c. $E(1, 4), F(5, -1)$

    d. $G(6, 5), H(6, -2)$

    e. $J(-3, -6), K(-2, 3)$

    f. $L(4, -9), M(6, -7)$

Chapters 1–3 Cumulative Test (continued)

12. Use the steps in the construction to explain how you know that $\overrightarrow{PQ}$ is perpendicular to $\overrightarrow{AB}$.

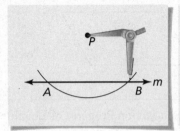 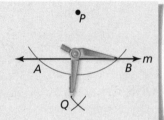 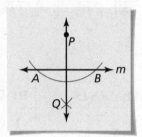

13. The equation of a line is $x + 3y = 12$.

   a. Use the numbers and symbols to create the equation of a line in slope-intercept form that passes through the point $(-3, 1)$ and is parallel to the given line.

   b. Use the numbers and symbols to create the equation of a line in slope-intercept form that passes through the point $(4, -2)$ and is perpendicular to the given line.

| x | y | $=$ | $+$ | $-$ | -14 | -2 |

| -1 | $-\frac{2}{3}$ | $-\frac{1}{3}$ | 1 | 2 | 3 | 10 |

14. Which of the following proves that two lines are parallel when the lines are cut by a transversal? Select all that apply.

   A. Alternate interior angles are congruent.

   B. Vertical angles are congruent.

   C. Consecutive interior angles are supplementary.

   D. Alternate exterior angles are congruent.

Chapters 1–3 **Cumulative Test** (continued)

15. Enter the reasons in the correct positions to complete the two-column proof.

Given $\angle 1 \cong \angle 2$, $m \parallel n$

Prove $\angle 3 \cong \angle 4$

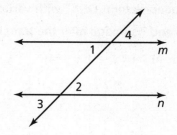

STATEMENTS	REASONS
1. $m \parallel n$	1. Given
2. $\angle 1 \cong \angle 2$	2. Given
3. $\angle 1 \cong \angle 4$	3.
4. $\angle 2 \cong \angle 3$	4.
5.	5. Substitution Property of Equality
6. $\angle 3 \cong \angle 4$	6.

16. You and your friend carpool to the soccer tournament. You meet at the halfway point between your houses first and then drive to the tournament. Each unit in the coordinate plane corresponds to 5 miles.

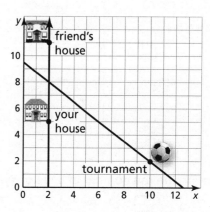

a. What are the coordinates of the midpoint of the line segment joining the two houses?

b. What is the distance that the two of you drive together?

Name _____ Date _____

Graph quadrilateral *QRST* with vertices $Q(-5, -1)$, $R(-3, 2)$, $S(2, 5)$, and $T(4, 0)$ and its image after the translation

Answers

1. **1.** $(x, y) \rightarrow (x - 3, y + 4)$

2. $(x, y) \rightarrow (x + 2, y)$

1. _____See left._____

2. _____See left._____

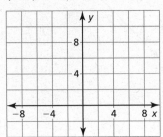

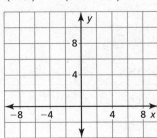

3. _____

4. _____

Find the component form of the vector that translates $P(4, 5)$ to P'.

5. _____See left._____

6. _____See left._____

3. $P'(-3, 7)$

4. $P'(-1, -6)$

7. _____

8. _____

Graph the polygon with the given vertices and its image after a reflection in the given line.

9. _____See left._____

10. _____See left._____

5. $A(-2, -1)$, $B(-3, 4)$, $C(5, 2)$; *y*-axis **6.** $D(-4, 2)$, $E(3, 6)$, $F(2, -2)$; $y = x$

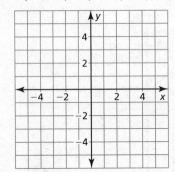

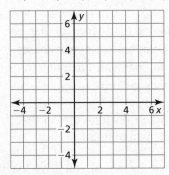

Determine the number of lines of symmetry for the figure.

7.

8.

Graph the polygon's image after a rotation of the given number of degrees clockwise about the origin.

9. $270°$

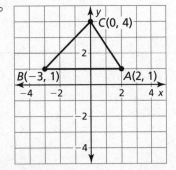

10. $180°$

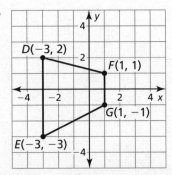

Chapter 4 Test A

Graph △*ABC* with vertices *A*(1, 2), *B*(−2, 0), and *C*(−2, 3) and its image after the translation.

1. $(x, y) \rightarrow (x + 1, y)$ **2.** $(x, y) \rightarrow (x - 2, y)$ **3.** $(x, y) \rightarrow (x + 3, y - 2)$

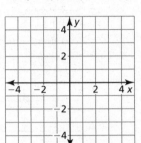 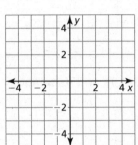 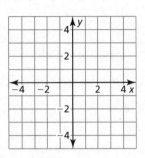

1.   __See left.__

2.   __See left.__

3.   __See left.__

4.   __See left.__

5.   __See left.__

Graph the polygon's image after a reflection in the given line.

4. $x = 2$ **5.** $y = -1$

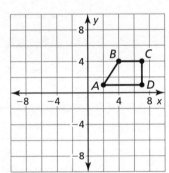 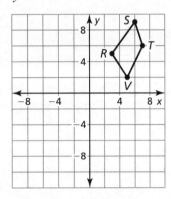

6. _____

7. _____

_____

8. _____

_____

_____

_____

9. _____

_____

_____

_____

10. _____

6. Identify the line symmetry (if any) of the word CHECKBOOK?

7. Trapezoid *JKLM* is rotated 180° clockwise about the origin. What are the new coordinates of *J′K′L′M′*?

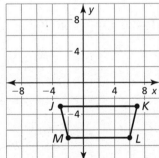

_____

_____

Determine whether the figure has rotational symmetry. If so, describe any rotations that map the figure onto itself.

8.   **9.**   **10.**

Chapter 4 **Test A** (continued)

Determine whether the polygons with the given verticies are congruent. Use transformations to explain your reasoining.

Answers

11. $A(8, -6)$, $B(1, -3)$, $C(1, -9)$ and $D(-7, 1)$, $E(0, -2)$, $F(0, 4)$

11. _____

_____

12. $J(-4, 1)$, $K(-10, 3)$, $L(-10, 9)$, $M(-4, 7)$, and $N(4, 2)$, $O(2, -8)$, $P(-4, -8)$, $Q(-2, 2)$

_____

_____

Graph △JKL with vertices J(3, 3), K(0, 0), and L(0, −3) and its image after a dilation with scale factor k.

_____

12. _____

13. $k = 3$

14. $k = \frac{1}{3}$

_____

_____

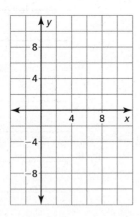

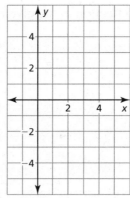

_____

13. __See left.__

14. __See left.__

15. _____

_____

15. △ABC has $m\angle A = 40°$ and $m\angle B = 60°$. △DEF has $m\angle D = 40°$ and $m\angle F = 80°$. Your partner concludes that the triangles are not similar. Do you agree or disagree? Why?

_____

16. _____

Describe a similarity transformation that maps the preimage to the image.

_____

16.

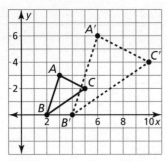

17.

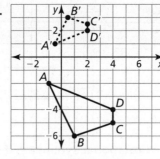

17. _____

_____

_____

Name_____ Date_____

Use the given translation to find the coordinates of the image of quadrilateral *ABCD*.   *Answers*

1. $(x, y) \rightarrow (x + 4), (y - 5)$ **2.** $(x, y) \rightarrow (x - 2), (y + 3)$

1. _____

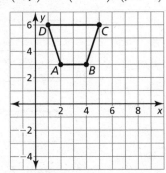   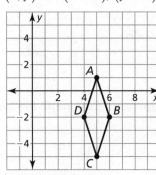

_____

2. _____

_____

3. _____

_____

Write a rule for the translation of the preimage to the image.   4. _____

5.   See left.

3   4.   6.   See left.

7. _____

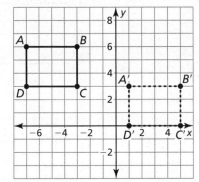   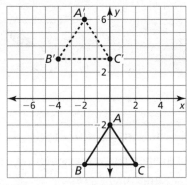

_____

_____

_____

8. _____

_____

Graph the polygon with the given vertices and its image after a rotation of the given number of degrees clockwise about the origin.   _____

5. $A(4, -1), B(4, -4), C(1, -4), D(1, -3);$ **6.** $D(3, 5), E(4, 1), F(1, 1); 270°$
    $180°$

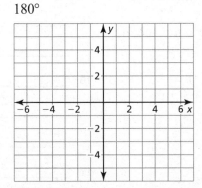   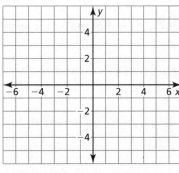

Determine whether the polygons with the given vertices are congruent or similar. Use transformations to explain your reasoning.

7. $A(-6, -3), B(-3, 7), C(2, 5)$ and $E(-7, -1), F(-4, 9), G(1, 7)$

8. $R(2, 3), S(2, -4), T(-4, 6), U(0, 6)$ and $M(9, 1), N(9, -20), O(-9, 10), P(3, 10)$

Chapter 4 **Test B** (continued)

Determine whether the object has line symmetry and whether it has rotational symmetry. Identify all lines of symmetry and angles of rotation that map the figure into itself.

9.

10.

11.

Describe a congruence transformation that maps the black perimage to the grey image.

12.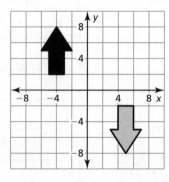

13.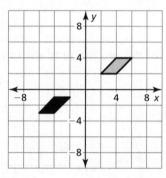

14. Consider triangle ABC with vertices $A(0, 0)$, $B(0, 4)$, $C(6, 0)$. The image of triangle ABC after a dilation has vertices $A'(0, 0)$, $B'(0, 10)$, $C'(15, 0)$. What is the scale factor of the dilation?

15. Triangle ABC with vertices $A(-2, 5)$, $B(1, 8)$, $C(7, 5)$ is dilated using a scale factor of $3\frac{1}{2}$. What are the coordinates of the image of triangle ABC?

Describe a similarity transformation that maps the first polygon to the second polygon.

16. $A(-6, -6)$, $B(-6, 3)$, $C(3, 3)$, $D(3, -6)$ and $J(-2, -2)$, $K(-2, 1)$, $L(1, 1)$, $M(1, -2)$

17. $A(1, 2)$, $B(2, 2)$, $C(1, 4)$ and $D(4, -6)$, $E(6, -6)$, $F(4, -2)$

Answers

9. _____

_____

_____

10. _____

_____

_____

_____

11. _____

_____

_____

_____

12. _____

_____

_____

13. _____

_____

_____

_____

14. _____

15. _____

_____

16. _____

_____

_____

17. _____

_____

_____

Chapter 4 — Alternative Assessment

1. The graph shows quadrilateral *ABCD*. Which set of vertices represents a rotation? a glide reflection? a translation? a similarity transformation? Write a rule for each of these transformations.

   a. $A'(-3, 1)$, $B'(-1, 4)$, $C'(-3, 6)$, $D'(-6, 3)$

   b. $A'(-5, -5)$, $B'(-3, -8)$, $C'(-5, -10)$, $D'(-8, -7)$

   c. $A'(-8, 0)$, $B'(-4, -6)$, $C'(-8, -10)$, $D'(-14, -4)$

   d. $A'(1, -3)$, $B'(4, -1)$, $C'(6, -3)$, $D'(3, -6)$

   e. $A'(-1, -3)$, $B'(-4, -1)$, $C'(-6, -3)$, $D'(-3, -6)$

   f. $A'(6, 1)$, $B'(8, 4)$, $C'(6, 6)$, $D'(3, 3)$

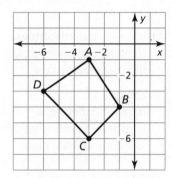

2. The vertices of a triangle are $Q(-2, 4)$, $R(2, 2)$, and $S(0, -2)$.

   a. Graph $\triangle QRS$.

   b. Describe a congruence transformation that that maps $\triangle QRS$ back to its original position. Use at least two different types of transformations.

   c. Describe and graph similarity transformation that maps each vertex of $\triangle QRS$ to Quadrant IV. Use at least two different types of transformations.

Chapter 4
Alternative Assessment Rubric

Score	Conceptual Understanding	Mathematical Skills	Work Habits
4	Show complete understanding of • translations, reflections, rotations, and dilations in the coordinate plane • congruence transformations and similarity transformations in the coordinate plane	Identifies and describes correctly all four transformations in Exercise 1. Graphs and describes correctly a congruence transformation and a similarity transformation that follow the given criteria.	Answers all parts of all problems. All graphs and transformations are drawn and explained carefully and thoroughly. Work is very neat and well organized.
3	Shows nearly complete understanding of • translations, reflections, rotations, and dilations in the coordinate plane • congruence transformations and similarity transformations in the coordinate plane	Identifies and describes correctly three transformations in Exercise 1. Graphs correctly but does not describe a congruence transformation and a similarity transformation that follow the given criteria	Answers most parts of all problems. Most graphs and transformations are drawn and explained carefully and thoroughly. Work is neat and organized.
2	Shows some understanding of • translations, reflections, rotations, and dilations in the coordinate plane • congruence transformations and similarity transformations in the coordinate plane	Identifies and describes correctly two transformations in Exercise 1. Graphs and/or describes incorrectly a congruence transformation and a similarity transformation that follow the given criteria.	Answers some parts of all problems. Some graphs and transformations are drawn or explained incorrectly. Work is not neat or organized.
1	Shows little understanding of • translations, reflections, rotations, and dilations in the coordinate plane • congruence transformations and similarity transformations in the coordinate plane	Identifies and describes correctly one or none of the transformations in Exercise 1. Does not graph or describe a congruence transformation and a similarity transformation that follow the given criteria.	Answers few parts of any problem. No graphs or transformations are drawn or explained. Work is sloppy and disorganized.

Name_____ Date _____

Performance Task

The Magic of Optics

Instructional Overview	
Launch Question	Look at yourself in a shiny spoon. What happens to your reflection? Can you describe this mathematically? Now turn the spoon over and look at your reflection on the back of it. What happens?
Summary	The inside of a spoon acts as a concave mirror, reducing and flipping the object of reflection. The back of a spoon acts as a convex mirror, which also shrinks the object of reflection but does not invert it.
	Students will hold a flat mirror a set distance from their face and examine their reflection. They will define and mark a key distance on the mirror (for example, from chin to eyebrow or from nose to hairline) and measure that distance. Students will make a rough sketch of their reflection on a coordinate plane.
	Then, holding the back of a spoon out the same distance from their face, students will mark and measure the same key distance on the spoon. The ratio of these measurements will give students the scale factor of the dilation. With this information, students can write the mathematical transformation. Using the transformation, students can sketch their transformed image.
	They then repeat this process with their image on the front of the spoon. This time, they must also consider how to represent their inverted image as part of the transformation.
	If time allows, the investigation can be repeated using different-size spoons to compare the scale factors.
Teacher Notes	This activity is best done in pairs or groups. One person can hold the spoon and mirror while the other marks. It will be important for the mirrors and spoons to be held at the same distance from the face at each measurement.
Supplies	Shiny, unscratched spoons; small, flat mirrors; rulers; string or measuring tape; markers that write on mirrors
Writing/Discussion Prompts	1. What is the center of dilation for your reflection in the spoon?
	2. Why was it important to hold the spoon and mirror the same distance from your face?

Performance Task (continued)

The Magic of Optics

Curriculum Content	
Content Objectives	• Represent in the coordinate plane reflections and dilations as seen in a mirror and a spoon. • Describe the reflections and dilations in the coordinate plane. • Determine the scale factors of the dilations and write the mathematical transformations.
Mathematical Practices	• Make sense of the problem and persevere in finding the scale factors of the dilations. • Use a coordinate plane to model the reflections and dilations.

Name_____ Date _____

Performance Task (continued)

Rubric

The Magic of Optics	Points	
Part 1: Features described and measurement given	**2** **1**	both are given only measurement is given
Part 2: Discussion of whether images are congruent or similar Explanation of first transformation (using back of spoon) Mathematical transformation $(x, y) \rightarrow (sx, sy)$ where s is scaling factor	**5** **3** **1**	well written and thorough, uses key words including *rigid motion*, dilation and numerical scaling factor are given, transformation is expressed mathematically writing is brief, scaling factor is given, transformation is expressed mathematically writing is brief, either scaling factor or transformation is given
Explanation of second transformation (using front of spoon) Mathematical transformation $(x, y) \rightarrow (-sx, -sy)$ where s is scaling factor	**5** **3** **1**	well written and thorough, uses key words including rigid motion, dilation, rotation, and numerical scaling factor are given, transformation is expressed mathematically writing is brief, scaling factor is given, transformation is expressed mathematically writing is brief, either scaling factor or transformation is given
Reflection sketches	**5** **3** **1**	all correct and drawn accurately one sketch not precise or incorrect two sketches not precise or incorrect
Mathematics Practice: Select one of the listed practices to evaluate. This component could be evaluated from observation of the student or a team working.	**3**	demonstration of the practice, partial credit can be awarded
Total Points	**20 points**	

Name _____ Date _____

The Magic of Optics

Look at yourself in a shiny spoon. What happens to your reflection? Can you describe this mathematically? Now turn the spoon over and look at your reflection on the back of it. What happens?

Part 1: The Baseline

Examine your reflection in a regular, flat mirror. Have your partner measure the distance from your face to the mirror and record the distance. Now, center your reflection in the mirror and have your partner mark a center point on the mirror. Note the distances between key features (for example, from your nose to your eyebrow or your lip to the bottom of your glasses). Have your partner mark this distance and record a description of the measurement. Using this measurement to guide you, sketch the key features of your face to scale on the coordinate axes using the marked center point as your origin.

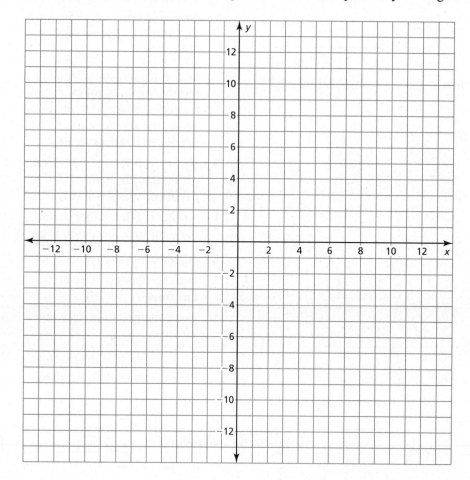

Chapter 4

Performance Task (continued)

The Magic of Optics

Part 2: The Transformation

1. Now, look at your reflection on the back of a shiny spoon, making sure you are holding the spoon the same distance from your face as you held the mirror. Center your reflection in the spoon as you did for the mirror and mark your origin. Mark and measure the same key features that you did using the flat mirror. Are the two measurements the same? Are your two reflections congruent or similar? Explain your reasoning.

2. Find a scaling factor for your reflection by taking the ratio of the measurements of your key features. Describe in words the transformation of your image from the mirror to the spoon. Now describe that transformation mathematically.
$$(x, y) \rightarrow (?, ?)$$

Using this transformation and your original sketch on the coordinate plane, sketch your reflection from the back of the spoon onto a coordinate plane.

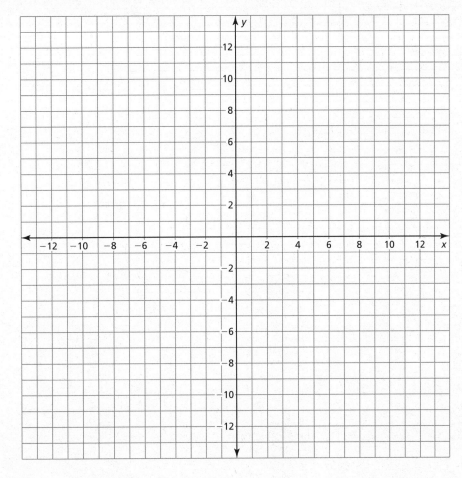

Name _____ Date _____

3. Extend your investigation by looking at your reflection on the front of the spoon.
   Repeat the measurement process as in Step 1. Compare this measurement with
   that taken with the flat mirror and the back of the spoon. What is the same? What
   additional transformation is taking place? Describe this in words and then
   mathematically. $(x, y) \rightarrow (?, ?)$

Using this transformation and your original sketch on the coordinate plane, sketch your
reflection from the spoon onto a coordinate plane.

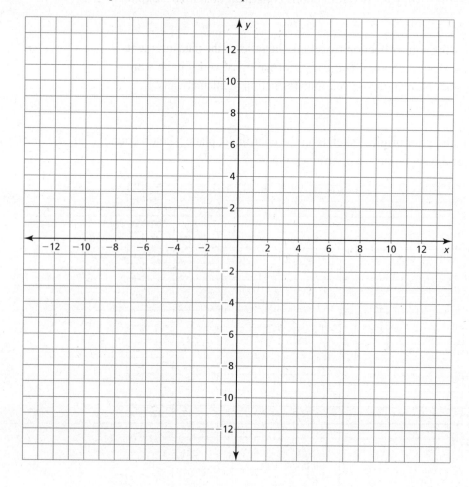

Name_____ Date _____

Performance Task (continued)

Teacher Notes:

Name _____ Date _____

Find the value of x and the measure of the exterior angle.

1.
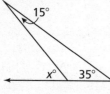
15°

x°   35°

2.
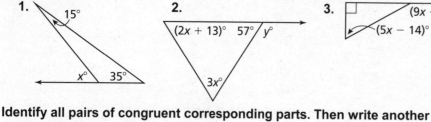
(2x + 13)° 57° y°

3x°

3.
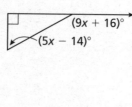
(9x + 16)°

(5x − 14)°

Answers

1. _____

_____

2. _____

_____

Identify all pairs of congruent corresponding parts. Then write another congruence statement for the polygons.

4. △DEF ≅ △LMN
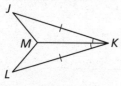
F   E   L

D   M   N

5. ABCD ≅ WXYZ
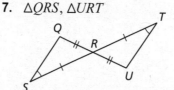
A   B   Z   W

D   C   Y   X

3. _____

_____

4. _____

_____

5. _____

Decide whether enough information is given to prove that the triangles are congruent using the SAS Congruence Theorem. Explain why or why not.

6. △JKM, △LKM
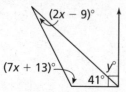
J

M   K

L

7. △QRS, △URT
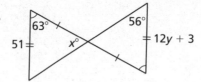
Q   T
R
S   U

_____

6. _____

_____

7. _____

Use the diagram to complete the statement. State which theorem you used.

8. If $\overline{LM} \cong \overline{LP}$, then ∠___ ≅ ∠___.

9. If ∠OMN ≅ ∠MNO, then ___ ≅ ___.

10. If $\overline{PN} \cong \overline{MP}$, then ∠___ ≅ ∠___.

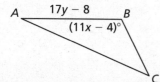
P   N

L

M   O

Find the values of x and y.

11.
(2x − 9)°

(7x + 13)°   y°
41°

12.
63°   56°
51   x°   12y + 3

13. △ABC ≅ △DEF

A   17y − 8   B
(11x − 4)°

C

F   D
23°
117°   12 + 13y

E

8. _____

_____

9. _____

_____

10. _____

_____

11. _____

_____

12. _____

_____

13. _____

_____

Chapter 5 Test A

Find the measure of the angle(s).

Answers

1.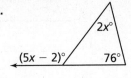

2.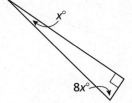

3.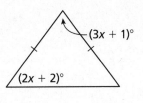

1. _____

2. _____

3. _____

4. _____

Classify the triangle by its sides and by the measure of its angles.

4.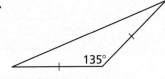

5.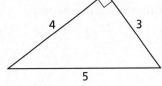

5. _____

6. _____

Name the corresponding parts, given △ALX ≅ △GIW.

7. _____

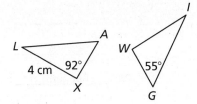

8. _____

9. _____

10. _____

11. _____

12. ___**See left.**___

6. $\overline{LX} \cong$ ___

7. $\angle I \cong$ ___

8. $\angle A \cong$ ___

9. $m\angle W =$ ___

10. $m\angle I =$ ___

11. $\triangle LAX \cong$ ___

12. Given $\overline{AB} \parallel \overline{CD}$ and $\overline{AB} \cong \overline{CD}$

Prove $\triangle ABC \cong \triangle DCB$

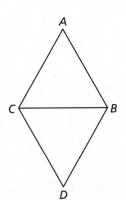

Chapter 5 **Test A** (continued)

Find the value of x.

13.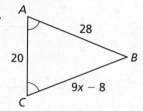

14.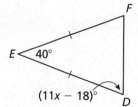

Answers

13. _____

14. _____

15. _____

_____

16. _____

_____

17. _____

18. _____

_____

19. ___See left.___

20. ___See left.___

Decide whether the triangles can be proven congruent by the given postulate or theorem. If not, state what information is needed.

15. $\triangle FLW \cong \triangle YLW$ by SAS

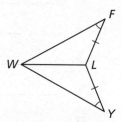

16. $\triangle TNS \cong \triangle UHS$ by AAS

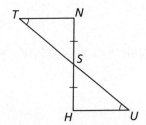

17. $\triangle IJH \cong \triangle KHJ$ by SSS

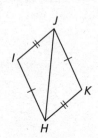

18. $\triangle TNS \cong \triangle UHS$ by HL

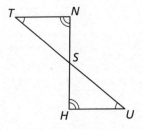

19. Explain how to prove $\angle CIR \cong \angle SIU$, given $\angle 1 \cong \angle 4$, $CU = RS$, and $IC = IS$.

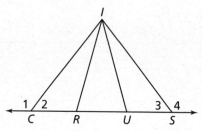

20. Given $\triangle ABC$ with $A(0, 0)$, $B(2, 3)$, and $C(4, 0)$, prove $\triangle ABC$ is isosceles.

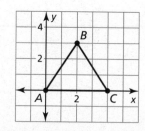

Name_____ Date_____

Classify each triangle by its sides and by the measure of its angles.

Answers

1.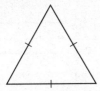

2.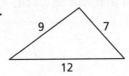

3.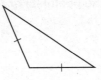

1. _____

2. _____

3. _____

4. _____

Find the value of x and the length of each side.

4.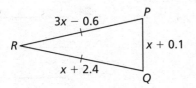

5.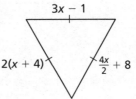

5. _____

6. _____

7. _____

8. _____

Given that PQRS ≅ WXYZ, find the corresponding parts.

9. _____

6. $\angle P \cong$ ___   7. $\overline{RS} \cong$ ___   8. $\overline{XY} \cong$ ___   9. $\angle Y \cong$ ___

10. _____

10. $\overline{PS} \cong$ ___   11. $\angle X \cong$ ___   12. $QPSR \cong$ ___   13. $YXWZ \cong$ ___

11. _____

12. _____

14. In $\triangle DEF$, find DE.

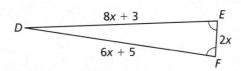

13. _____

14. _____

15. One of the acute angles in a right triangle has a measure of $35°$. What is the measure of the other acute angle?

15. _____

16. _____

17. _____

16. The vertex angle of an isosceles triangle is $58°$. What are the measures of the base angles?

18. _____

19. _____

Find the measure of the missing angles.

20. _____

17. $m\angle 1$

21. _____

18. $m\angle 2$

19. $m\angle 3$

20. $m\angle 4$

21. $m\angle 5$

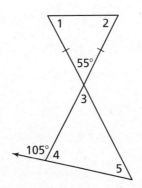

Chapter 5 **Test B** (continued)

Decide whether the triangles can be proven congruent by a postulate or theorem. If they can, state the postulate or theorem that can be used.

Answers

22.

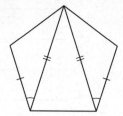

23.

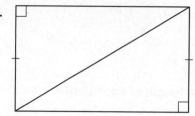

24.

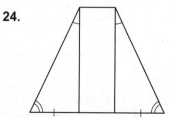

25.

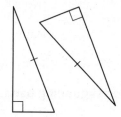

22. _____

_____

23. _____

_____

24. _____

_____

25. _____

_____

26. ___See left.___

27. ___See left.___

Use the diagram to write a two-column proof.

26. **Given** $\overrightarrow{OM}$ bisects $\angle AOB$ and $\overrightarrow{MO}$ bisects $\angle AMB$

   Prove $\triangle AMO \cong \triangle BMO$

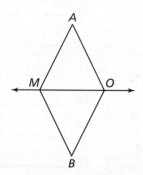

27. **Given** $AB = AC$ and $\angle BAD \cong \angle CAD$

   Prove $BD = CD$

Alternative Assessment

1. On a calendar, each day is represented by a rectangle. To keep track of the date, you cross off the previous day by connecting one pair of opposite corners of the rectangle, as shown.

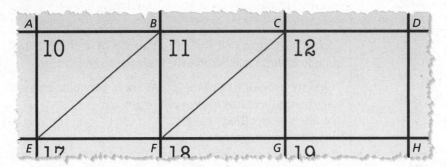

   a. Classify △*ABE* by its sides and by measuring its angles. Explain your reasoning.

   b. List the five triangle congruence theorems.

   c. For each of the triangle congruence theorems you listed in part (b), prove that △*FBC* ≅ △*CGF* using that theorem. (You will need to write five different proofs.)

Name _____ Date _____

Score	Conceptual Understanding	Mathematical Skills	Work Habits
4	Shows complete understanding of: • types of triangles • congruent triangles • the five triangle congruence theorems	Correctly classifies the specified triangle by its sides and angles Correctly identifies all five triangle congruence theorems Correctly uses all five triangle congruence theorems to prove that the two specified triangles are congruent	Answers all parts of the problem Answers are explained thoroughly with mathematical terminology. Work is very neat and well organized.
3	Shows nearly complete understanding of: • types of triangles • congruent triangles • the five triangle congruence theorems	Correctly classifies the specified triangle by its sides and angles Correctly identifies four triangle congruence theorems Correctly uses four triangle congruence theorems to prove that the two specified triangles are congruent	Answers most parts of the problem Answers are explained with mathematical terminology. Work is neat and organized.
2	Shows some understanding of: • types of triangles • congruent triangles • the five triangle congruence theorems	Incorrectly classifies the specified triangle by its sides and angles Correctly identifies two or three triangle congruence theorems Correctly uses two or three triangle congruence theorems to prove that the two specified triangles are congruent	Answers some parts of the problem Answers are poorly or incorrectly explained. Work is not very neat or organized.
1	Shows little understanding of: • types of triangles • congruent triangles • the five triangle congruence theorems	Does not classify the specified triangle by its sides and angles Correctly identifies zero or one triangle congruence theorem Correctly uses zero or one triangle congruence theorems to prove that the two specified triangles are congruent	Answers few parts of the problem No explanation is included with answers. Work is sloppy and disorganized.

Name_____ Date_____

Chapter 5 **Performance Task**

Creating the Logo

Instructional Overview	
Launch Question	Congruent triangles are often used to create company logos. Why are they used and what are the properties that make them attractive? Following the required constraints, create your new logo and justify how your shape contains the required properties.
Summary	Students will use any method to create logos based on criteria from this chapter. They will be asked to describe their creation using terminology from the chapter. There are some required shapes, and then students can add as many as they wish. Students' final task will be to construct two congruent shapes and describe how they would prove the congruence.
Teacher Notes	This assessment will let you know if the students understand the terminology and can create images that fit the criteria. Students will first look for logos that are in use and then create their own. In the final step, you can have students use dynamic geometry software or a compass and straightedge.
Supplies	Handout, compass and straightedge and/or dynamic geometry tool
Mathematical Discourse	What are the most important components of a logo, and why does it matter?
Writing/Discussion Prompts	1. Why do companies need a logo? 2. What geometric shapes are used most often in logos? Why do you think that is? Provide an example.

Name _____ Date _____

Performance Task (continued)

Creating the Logo

Curriculum Content	
Content Objectives	• In the most precise terms, describe geometric shapes found in company logos. • Construct a logo using a straightedge and compass or dynamic geometry software and justify that the construction meets the given criteria.
Mathematical Practices	• Use geometric shapes to model company logos. • Use tools, such as a straightedge and compass or dynamic geometry software, to construct a company logo.

Rubric

Creating the Logo	Points
1 Students find three logos and use correct terminology to describe each one.	**6** Total possible points **1** for each logo sketched **1** for each logo description
2 Creations included all of the required criteria: Name, two equilateral triangles, one scalene triangle, two isosceles triangles, and one obtuse triangle.	**14** Total possible points **1** for the name of the company **1** for sketching a logo **1** for each of the 6 shapes included in the logo **1** for each correct label/description of the 6 shapes
3 Constructions are correct and contain the required congruent shapes. The student's method of proving triangle congruence is provided with specific terminology.	**6** Triangles are constructed correctly and a valid method of proof is described **4** Construction is correct but method of proof is not described **2** Construction is created with minor errors as well as errors in the description
Mathematics Practice: Model with mathematics and use appropriate tools strategically.	**2** The tools are used correctly and the logos are modeled using the given constraints. Partial credit can be awarded.
Total Points	**28 points**

Name_____ Date_____

Creating the Logo

Congruent triangles are often used to create company logos. Why are they used and what are the properties that make them attractive? Following the constraints given, create your new logo and justify how your shape contains the required properties.

1. Find three different examples of company logos that include basic shapes. Write the name and sketch the logo. Use terminology from this chapter to describe a triangle used in each one.

2. Create a name and logo for your own company. Your logo must contain at least two equilateral triangles, one scalene triangle, two isosceles triangles, and one obtuse triangle. Draw the logo and correctly label and describe each of your triangles.

3. Use a straightedge and a compass (or computer software) to construct a logo with at least two congruent triangles. Describe the method you could use to prove your triangles are congruent. In your description, use specific terminology to classify your new triangles.

Name _____ Date _____

Quiz
For use after Section 6.3

Find the indicated measure.

1. *BC*

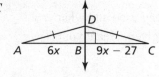

2. *m∠KJL*

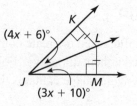

Answers

1. _____

2. _____

3. a. _____

b. _____

4. a. _____

b. _____

5. _____

6. _____

7. _____

8. _____

9. _____

_____

10. _____

_____

11. _____

12. _____

13. _____

Tell whether the information in the diagram allows you to conclude that (a) point *D* **lies on the perpendicular bisector of** $\overline{BC}$ **or that (b)** $\overline{AD}$ **bisects** $\angle BAC$.

3.

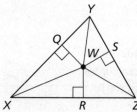

4.

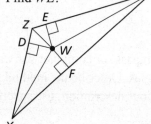

Use the given vertices of the triangle, find the coordinates of the following:

5. Circumcenter: $M(4, 0)$, $N(-2, 4)$, $O(0, 6)$

6. Centroid: $A(1, 2)$, $B(3, 4)$, $C(5, 0)$

The incenter of $\triangle XYZ$ **is point** *W***. Use the given information to find the indicated measure.**

7. $SW = 5x$

$WR = 3x + 18$

Find QW.

8. $DW = 7x - 13$

$FW = 15x - 37$

Find WE.

Tell whether the orthocenter is *inside*, *on*, **or** *outside* **the triangle. Then find its coordinates.**

9. $L(-2, 5)$, $M(6, 5)$, $N(4, -1)$ **10.** $M(4, -3)$, $N(8, 5)$, $O(8, -8)$

Complete the statement with *always*, *sometimes*, **or** *never*.

11. The centroid is _____ inside the triangle.

12. The orthocenter is _____ inside an obtuse triangle.

13. The centroid, circumcenter, and orthocenter are _____ the same point.

Chapter 6 **Test A**

Find the measure.

1. *PQ*

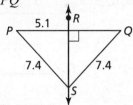

2. *JM*

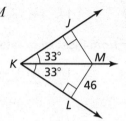

Answers

1. _____

2. _____

3. _____

4. _____

5. _____

   _____

6. _____

7. _____

8. _____

   _____

   _____

   _____

9. _____

10. _____

11. _____

Use the diagram to find the indicated angle measure.

3. Given $m\angle B = 57°$, $m\angle C = 51°$, and $\overline{AD}$ bisects $\angle BAC$, find $m\angle ADC$.

4. Given $m\angle B = 66°$, $m\angle BAD = 34°$, and $\overline{AD}$ bisects $\angle BAC$, find $m\angle DAC$.

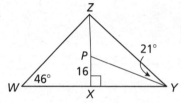

5. $\overline{PZ}$ and $\overline{PY}$ are angle bisectors of $\triangle WYZ$. Find the measure of $\angle WZP$ and the distance from P to $\overline{YZ}$.

6. Find the circumcenter of $\triangle ABC$ with vertices $A(12, 0)$, $B(0, -6)$, and $C(0, 0)$.

7. Your friend is trying to balance a triangle on the tip of his pencil. Find the coordinates on the centroid if the triangle has vertices of $(2, 4)$, $(10, 6)$, and $(12, -10)$.

8. In $\triangle PQR$, $SP = 78$, and $UM = 19$. Find SM, MR, and UR.

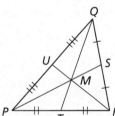

Find the missing length indicated.

9. *CD*

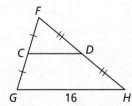

10. *SR*

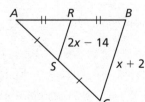

11. *TS*

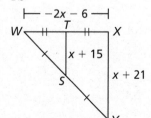

Name _____ Date _____

Tell whether a triangle can have sides with given lengths. Explain.

12. 4, 7, 10   **13.** 2, 9, 12   **14.** 14, 18, 32   **15.** 103, 41.9, 62.5

List the angles of △*JKL* **in order from least to greatest.**

16. $J(-3, -2)$, $K(3, 6)$, $L(8, -2)$ **17.** $J(10, -4)$, $K(5, 3)$, $L(2, -8)$

Compare the given measures.

18. *TU* and *SV*

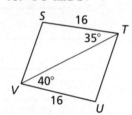

19. $m\angle GHJ$ and $m\angle KLM$

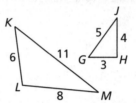

20. *AC* and *XZ*

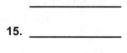

Write and solve an inequality for the possible values of x.

21.   **22.**   **23.**

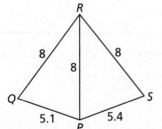

Complete the statement with <, >, or =.

24. $m\angle QRP$ _____ $m\angle SRP$ **25.** $m\angle QPR$ _____ $m\angle QRP$

26. $m\angle PRS$ _____ $m\angle RSP$ **27.** $m\angle RSP$ _____ $m\angle RPS$

Answers

12. _____

_____

13. _____

_____

14. _____

_____

15. _____

_____

16. _____

17. _____

18. _____

19. _____

20. _____

21. _____

22. _____

23. _____

24. _____

25. _____

26. _____

27. _____

Chapter 6 Test B

Find the length of *AC*.

1. *AB* = 18.5, *AX* = 8.1, and *BC* = 18.5

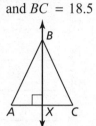

2. *AB* = 9, *AX* = 4, and *BC* = 9

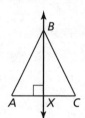

Find the indicated measure.

3. *DY*

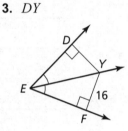

4. *m∠DEY*

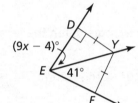

5. *m∠DEF*

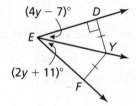

1. _____

2. _____

3. _____

4. _____

5. _____

6. __See left.__

7. _____

8. _____

9. _____

10. _____

11. _____

6. A school district is planning to build a playground on the school's campus. They want the playground to be the same distance from the elementary school *E*, the middle school *M*, and the high school *H*. Draw a sketch on the diagram to show where the playground should be placed.

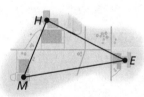

$\overline{PF}$ and $\overline{QF}$ are angle bisectors of △*PQR*. Find each measure.

7. distance from *F* to $\overline{PQ}$

8. *m∠FQP*

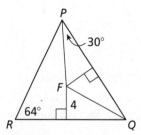

Find the following coordinates of △*ABC* with vertices *A*(−4, 6), *B*(2, 6), and *C*(−4, −2).

9. circumcenter   10. orthocenter   11. centroid

Chapter 6 Test B (continued)

Find the coordinates of the vertices of the midsegment of a triangle for a triangle with the given vertices.

12. $A(-2, -4)$, $B(4, 8)$, $C(6, -2)$ **13.** $A(4, 5)$, $B(-2, -7)$, $C(-8, 3)$

$\overline{DE}$ is a midsegment of $\triangle ABC$. Find the value of n.

14. 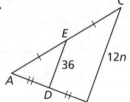   **15.** 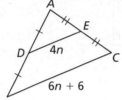   **16.**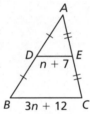

Describe the possible lengths of the third side of the triangle given the lengths of the other two sides.

17. 5 yd, 24 yd   **18.** 8.7 in., 3.2 in.   **19.** 4.16 m, 2 m

List the angles of $\triangle DEF$ in order from least to greatest.

20. $D(-2, -3)$, $E(6, 3)$, $F(-2, 8)$ **21.** $D(2, 5)$, $E(2, -5)$, $F(4, 6)$

Copy and complete the statement with <, >, or =.

22. PS ___ RS **23.** $m\angle BCA$ ___ $m\angle DCA$

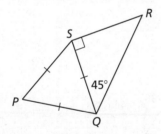   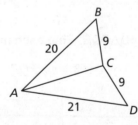

24. Write an indirect proof that a triangle cannot contain more than one obtuse angle.

Answers

12. _____

13. _____

14. _____

15. _____

16. _____

17. _____

18. _____

19. _____

20. _____

21. _____

22. _____

23. _____

24.   **See left.**

Name_____ Date _____

Chapter 6

1. You are making a blueprint to show the features being added at a scenic gardens park. The figure shows the layout of the gardens in a coordinate plane.

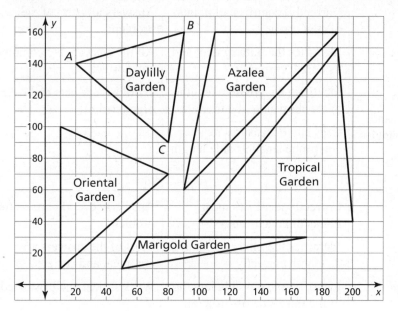

a. A water fountain will be placed at the orthocenter of the tropical garden. Approximate the coordinates of this point.

b. A path will cut through the Azalea Garden so that it is the midsegment of the side of the garden that is parallel to the horizontal axis. Find the coordinates of the endpoints of the segment that represents the path.

c. Find the length of the path that will cut through the Azalea Garden.

d. A statue will be placed at the incenter of the Azalea Garden. Approximate the coordinates of this point.

e. A triangular goldfish pond will be built at the centroid of the Oriental Garden. Approximate the coordinates of this point.

f. The lengths of two sides of the triangular goldfish pond will be 3 feet and 4 feet. Describe the possible lengths of the third side.

g. In the Daylily Garden, $m\angle A \approx 56°$ and $m\angle C \approx 58°$. Which is the shortest side of the Daylily Garden? Explain.

h. A bench is to be installed at one of the points of concurrency of the Marigold Garden. From which point, the *circumcenter*, *incenter*, *centroid*, or *orthocenter*, is it possible to view the greatest portion of all the gardens without looking more than 90° to the right or left? Explain.

Name _____ Date _____

Score	Conceptual Understanding	Mathematical Skills	Work Habits
4	Shows complete understanding of: • points of concurrency for triangles • triangle midsegments • ordering side lengths and angle measures in triangles • the Triangle Inequality Theorem (Theorem 6.11)	Correctly identifies all points of concurrency Identifies the midsegment and its length correctly Identifies the possible lengths of the third side of a triangle Uses angle measures to determine smallest side length	Answers all parts of the problem All the answers are complete and correct. Work is very neat and well organized.
3	Shows nearly complete understanding of: • points of concurrency for triangles • triangle midsegments • ordering side lengths and angle measures in triangles • the Triangle Inequality Theorem (Theorem 6.11)	Correctly identifies most points of concurrency Identifies the midsegment and its length correctly Identifies the possible lengths of the third side of a triangle Uses angle measures to determine smallest side length	Answers several parts of the problem Most of the answers are complete and correct. Work is neat and organized.
2	Shows some understanding of: • points of concurrency for triangles • triangle midsegments • ordering side lengths and angle measures in triangles • the Triangle Inequality Theorem (Theorem 6.11)	Incorrectly identifies many points of concurrency Misidentifies the midsegment or its length May incorrectly identify possible lengths of third side Show incomplete understanding of angle/side length relationships	Answers some parts of the problems Many of the answers are incomplete or incorrect. Work is not very neat or organized.
1	Shows little understanding of: • points of concurrency for triangles • triangle midsegments • ordering side lengths and angle measures in triangles • the Triangle Inequality Theorem (Theorem 6.11)	Incorrectly identifies most or all points of concurrency Misidentifies the midsegment or its length Incorrectly identifies possible lengths of third side Shows poor understanding of angle/side relationships	Provides very few answers for the problem Almost none of the answers are correct. Work is sloppy and disorganized.

Name_____ Date _____

Bicycle Renting Stations

Instructional Overview	
Launch Question	The city planners for a large town want to add bicycle renting stations around downtown. How will you decide the best locations? Where will you place the rental stations based on the ideas of the city planners?
Summary	This activity is a review of the definitions and constructions in the chapter. It highlights the options for creating different points and asks students to make decisions on which might be the best location.
Teacher Notes	Make sure your students have the construction tools needed, along with a copy of the 'city'. The students will be asked to describe the construction, name the center, and create the construction. You could display this on dynamic geometry software and work through the activity electronically as well.
Supplies	Handout, compass and straightedge, and/or dynamic geometry software
Mathematical Discourse	Do you think there are discussions about where to locate new things in a city or town? Why might a business either want something close to it or maybe have it located in another part of town.
Writing/Discussion Prompts	1. Provide an example of something new in a town. Describe a business that might want it to be located close to it and why. Describe a business that might not want it to be in its neighborhood and why. 2. For each of the following mathematics centers of a triangle, describe a real-world situation that would use each center; circumcenter, incenter, orthocenter, and centroid.

Curriculum Content	
Content Objectives	• Use construction methods to find the circumcenter, the incenter, and the centroid of a triangle.
Mathematical Practices	• Make sense of how constructing the circumcenter, the incenter, and the centroid of a triangle can lead to a solution to the problem. • Look for and make use of the points of concurrency, the circumcenter, the incenter, and the centroid of a triangle, to solve a problem.

Rubric

Bicycle Renting Stations	Points
1. Students construct the circumcenter. The circumcenter is the intersection of the perpendicular bisectors of the sides of the triangle. 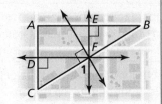	**18 total** **6** The construction of the location is described correctly and named, the construction is correct **4** Construction is correct but the steps are not clear in the writing **2** Location is named but there are errors in construction **1** A correct start
2. Students construct the incenter. The incenter is the intersection of the angle bisectors of the triangle. 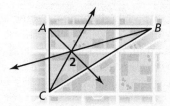	
3. Students construct the centroid. The centroid is the intersection of the medians of the triangle. 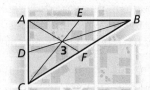	
4: Students provide a clear explanation of their choice; any one of the points could be correct. *Sample answer:* To avoid the appearance that one business is being preferred over the others, the city planners might decide to place the charging/rental station at the circumcenter, which is the same distance from each of the three businesses.	**4** Choice of location is made and the description contains an explanation in terms of mathematics and the situation **2** A choice is made yet the explanation does not include mathematics **1** Choice made
Mathematics Practice: Problem solving and use of mathematical structure are demonstrated through the activity.	**3** Students persevere to the end and use the structure of triangles to find the correct location
Total Points	**25 points**

Name_____ Date_____

Bicycle Renting Stations

The city planners for a large town want to add bicycle renting stations around downtown. How will you decide the best locations? Where will you place the rental stations based on the ideas of the city planners?

Use the information you have learned in this chapter to find the best location based on the teams' suggestions. Describe your steps on the next page using the geometric terms from the chapter. Construct your locations on the large map on the final page.

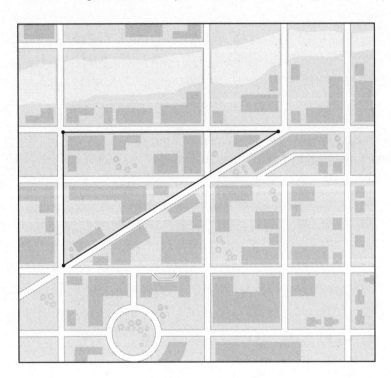

Performance Task (continued)

Bicycle Renting Stations

1. The first team of planners thinks that the charging/rental station should be equidistant from the three largest businesses represented by black points. Label this Location 1. Describe your steps.

2. Team two proposes that the charging/rental station should be equidistant from the three roads that join the businesses represented by black points. Label this Location 2. Describe your steps.

3. The third team proposes that the location be at the centroid of the triangle formed by the three largest businesses. Label this Location 3. Describe your steps

Name_____ Date _____

Bicycle Renting Stations

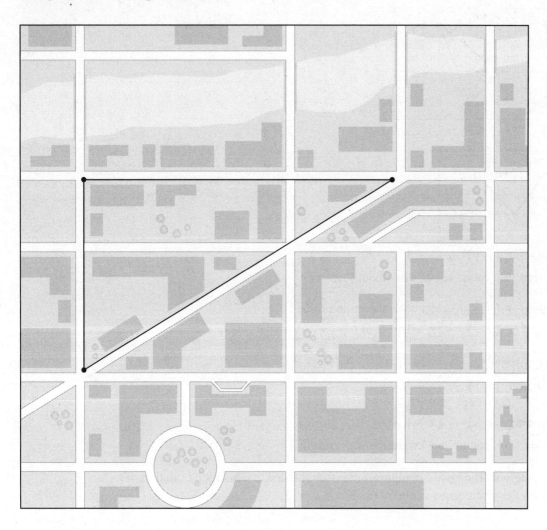

4. Which location do you believe would be the best? Explain why in terms of
   geometry and city planning.

Chapters 4–6 **Cumulative Test**

1. Which composition of transformations maps $\triangle ABC$ to $\triangle DEF$?

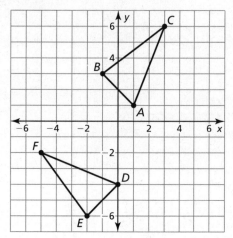

   A. Translation: $(x, y) \rightarrow (x + 1, y - 5)$
      Rotation: 90° counterclockwise about the origin

   B. Rotation: 90° counterclockwise about the origin
      Translation: $(x, y) \rightarrow (x - 1, y - 5)$

   C. Rotation: 90° counterclockwise about the origin
      Translation: $(x, y) \rightarrow (x + 1, y - 5)$

   D. Translation: $(x, y) \rightarrow (x - 1, y - 5)$
      Rotation: 90° counterclockwise about the origin

2. Copy the diagram. Then use a compass and a straightedge to construct a dilation of
   $\triangle FGH$ with the given center C and scale factor $k = 2$.

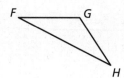

   $C \bullet$

Chapters 4–6 **Cumulative Test** (continued)

3. Graph the directed line segment $\overline{VW}$ with endpoints $V(-2, 3)$ and $W(3, 8)$. Then find the coordinates of point Y along with the directed line segment $\overline{VW}$ so that the ratio of $\overline{VY}$ to $\overline{YW}$ is 3 to 2.

4. The graph shows quadrilateral *ABCD* and quadrilateral *PQRS*.

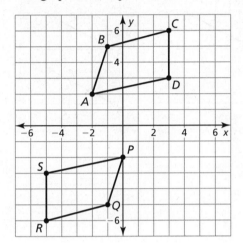

   a. Write a composition of transformations that maps quadrilateral *ABCD* to quadrilateral *PQRS*.

   b. Are the quadrilaterals congruent? Explain your reasoning.

5. Which equation represents the line passing through the point $(4, -5)$ that is perpendicular to the line $y = -2x + 7$?

   A. $y = \frac{1}{2}x - 7$

   B. $y = -2x + 3$

   C. $y = \frac{1}{2}x - 3$

   D. $y = -2x - 13$

6. Which scale factor(s) would create a dilation of $\overline{PQ}$ that is longer than $\overline{PQ}$? Select all that apply.

| 1 | $\frac{1}{2}$ | $\frac{1}{4}$ | 2 | $\frac{3}{4}$ | $\frac{6}{5}$ | 3 | $\frac{5}{2}$ |

Cumulative Test (continued)

7. Your friend claims that the Triangle Sum Theorem (Theorem 5.1) can be used to prove the Third Angles Theorem (Theorem 5.4). Is your friend correct? Explain your reasoning.

8. Use the steps in the construction to explain how you know that ∠EDF ≅ ∠BAC.

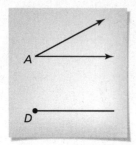 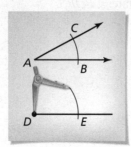 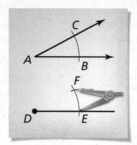 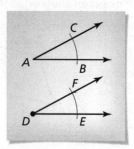

9. The graph shows △ABC and △RST.

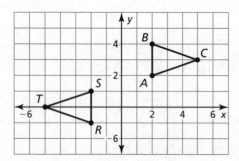

   a. Write a composition of transformations that maps △ABC to △RST.

   b. Is the composition a congruence transformation? If so, identify all congruent corresponding parts.

Chapters 4–6 **Cumulative Test** (continued)

10. The graph shows △*TUV* and △*XYZ*.

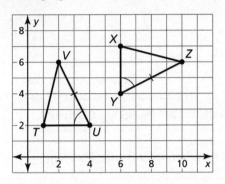

a. Prove △*TUV* ≅ △*XYZ*.

b. Describe the composition of rigid motions that maps △*TUV* to △*XYZ*.

11. Which figure(s) have rotational symmetry? Select all that apply.

A.    B.   C. 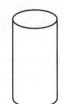   D.

12. Write a coordinate proof.

Given Coordinates of vertices of triangle *ABC*

Prove Triangle *ABC* is an isosceles triangle.

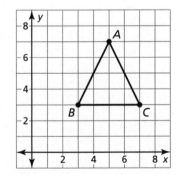

Name _____ Date _____

13. Which definition(s) and/or theorem(s) can you use to prove the Triangle Inequality Theorem (Theorem 6.11)? Select all that apply.

    Given △ABC

    Prove AB + BC > AC

    | Angle Addition Postulate (Postulate 1.4) |

    | Perpendicular Bisector Theorem (Theorem 6.1) |

    | Triangle Longer Side Theorem (Theorem 6.9) |

    | Substitution Property of Equality |

    | Triangle Larger Angle Theorem (Theorem 6.10) |

    | Segment Addition Postulate (Postulate 1.2) |

14. Use the figure to write a two-column proof.

    Given $\overline{BD}$ is the perpendicular bisector of $\overline{AC}$.

    Prove $\overline{BA} \cong \overline{BC}$

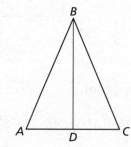

15. What are the coordinates of the orthocenter of △PQR?

    A. (2, 2)

    B. $\left(\frac{5}{2}, 2\right)$

    C. (3, 2)

    D. $\left(\frac{7}{2}, 2\right)$

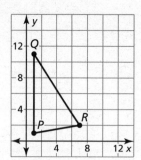

Chapters 4–6 **Cumulative Test** (continued)

16. Use of the graph of △*FGH*.

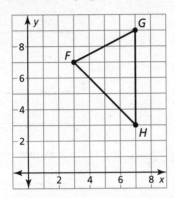

   a. Find the coordinates of the circumcenter of △*FGH*.

   b. Find the equation of the line that goes through the circumcenter and is perpendicular to $\overline{FG}$.

17. A triangle has vertices $A(-3, -4)$, $B(1, 3)$, and $C(3, -4)$. Your friend claims that a reflection in the *y*-axis and a dilation by a scale factor of $\frac{1}{2}$ will produce a similarity transformation. Is your friend correct? Explain your reasoning.

18. The graph shows a rotation of 180° of quadrilateral *ABCD* about the origin. Show that the line containing points *A* and *C* is parallel to the line containing points *A′* and *C′*.

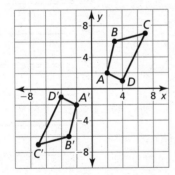

Name _____ Date _____

Find the sum of the measures of the interior angles of the indicated convex polygon.

Answers

1. hexagon   **2.** 17-gon   **3.** 24-gon

1. _____

2. _____

Find the value of x.

3. _____

4.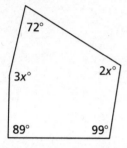

5.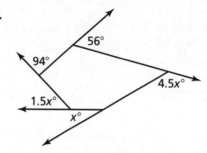

4. _____

5. _____

6. _____

_____

Find the measure of each interior angle and each exterior angle of the indicated regular polygon.

7. _____

6. nonagon   **7.** 25-gon

_____

8. _____

Find the indicated measure in □ABCD.

9. _____

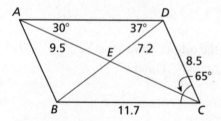

10. _____

11. _____

12. _____

13. _____

8. AD   **9.** BA   **10.** m∠BEC

14. _____

11. m∠ABC   **12.** m∠ACD   **13.** m∠DBA

_____

_____

State which theorem you can use to show that the quadrilateral is a parallelogram. Explain your reasoning.

15. _____

14.    **15.**

_____

_____

94 **Geometry**
Assessment Book

Chapter 7 Test A

Find the sum of the measures of the interior angles and the sum of the measures of the exterior angles of the polygon.

Answers

1.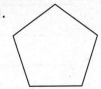

2.

3.

1. _____
   _____

2. _____
   _____

3. _____

Find the value of *x*.

4.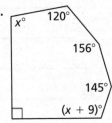

5.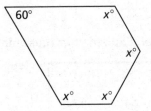

4. _____

5. _____

6. _____

7. _____

6. Find the measure of each exterior angle of a regular polygon in which the sum of the measures of the interior angles is 5400°.

8. _____

7. What is the sum of the exterior angles in a regular 15-gon?

   _____

Find the indicated measure in □*ABCD*. Explain your reasoning.

9. _____

8. *AD*

   _____

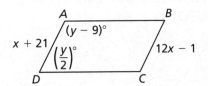

9. *m∠B*

10. _____

11. _____

   _____

10. Three vertices of parallelogram *DEFG* are *D*(5, 2), *E*(2, 6), and *F*(−8, −3). Find the coordinates of vertex *G*.

12. _____

   _____

Find the indicated measure in parallelogram *STUV*. Explain your reasoning.

13. _____

11. *TS*   12. *SW*

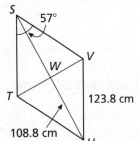

14. _____

13. *m∠SVU*   14. *m∠STU*

15. _____

15. *US*   16. *m∠TUV*

   _____

16. _____

   _____

Name _____ Date _____

Find the values of *x* and *y* that make the quadrilateral a parallelogram.

Answers

17.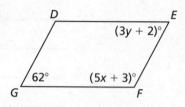

18.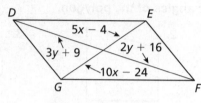

17. _____

18. _____

19. _____

19. Show that the quadrilateral with vertices $B(-4, 4)$, $D(6, 6)$, $F(7, 0)$, and $H(-3, -2)$ is a parallelogram.

_____

_____

_____

Classify the special quadrilateral. Explain your reasoning.

20.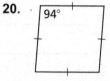

21.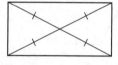

22.

20. _____

_____

The diagonals of rhombus *ABCD* intersect at *E*.
Given that $m\angle CAD$ is 20° and $CE = 4$, find
the indicated measure.

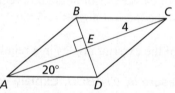

21. _____

23. $m\angle BCA$ 24. $m\angle CDA$ 25. AC

_____

22. _____

Determine whether the given points represent the vertices of a trapezoid.
If so, determine whether it is isosceles or not.

23. _____

26. $A(-4, -1)$, $B(-4, 6)$, $C(2, 6)$, $D(2, -4)$

24. _____

27. $A(-5, 2)$, $B(-5, 6)$, $C(-1, 6)$, $D(2, -1)$

25. _____

26. _____

Find the length of the midsegment of the trapezoid.

28.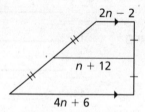

29.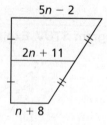

27. _____

28. _____

29. _____

In kite *ABCD*, $m\angle DAE = 16°$, and $m\angle EDC = 64°$. Find the indicated
measure.

30. _____

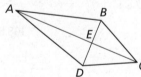

30. $m\angle ABC$

31. _____

31. $m\angle BCD$

Name_____ Date_____

A window is the shape of a quadrilateral. Find the indicated measure.

Answers

1. $m\angle A$

2. $m\angle B$

3. $m\angle C$

4. $m\angle D$

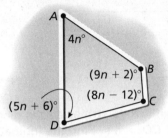

1. _____

2. _____

3. _____

4. _____

5. _____

5. Find the measure of each interior angle of a regular dodecagon.

6. _____

6. Find the measure of each exterior angle of a regular 16-gon.

7. _____

In parallelogram *EFGH*, *EH* = 16, *HZ* = 4, and *m∠EHG* = 44°. Find the indicated measure.

8. _____

7. *FH*

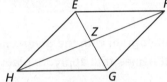

9. _____

8. *m∠FEH*

10. _____

Find the values of *x* and *y* that make the quadrilateral a parallelogram.

11. _____

9.

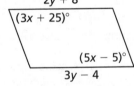

10.

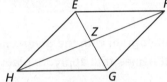

12. _____

State which theorem you can use to show that the quadrilateral is a parallelogram. Explain your reasoning.

13. _____

11. $a = 6$ and $b = 4.5$

12. $a = 12$ and $b = 11.5$

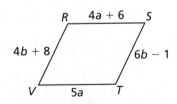

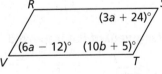

14. _____

From the information given, can you determine whether the quadrilateral is a parallelogram? Explain your reasoning.

15. _____

13.

14.

15.

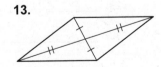

Chapter 7 **Test B** (continued)

Given the most specific name for the quadrilateral. Explain your reasoning.

16.
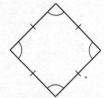

17.
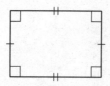

18.

Answers

16. _____

_____

17. _____

_____

18. _____

_____

19. _____

20. _____

21. _____

22. _____

23. _____

The flag of Scotland is a rectangle with white stripes as the diagonals. In rectangle *SCOT*, *SO* = 92.4, and *CO* = 41. Find the indicated measure.

19. *OL*   **20.** *ST*

21. *CT*   **22.** *LT*

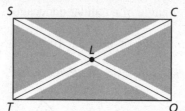

Determine whether the parallelogram with the given vertices is a *rectangle*, *rhombus*, or *square*. Give all names that apply. Explain your reasoning.

23. $A(-6, -2)$, $B(-3, 3)$, $C(2, 0)$, $D(-1, -5)$

24. $L(-3, 4)$, $M(3, 3)$, $N(4, -3)$, $O(-2, -2)$

In kite *EFGH*, $m\angle FHG = 15°$, and $m\angle FEH = 146°$. Find the indicated measure.

25. $m\angle FEJ$

26. $m\angle EHJ$

27. $m\angle FGJ$

28. $m\angle EHG$

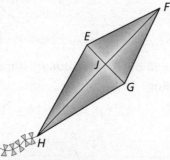

24. _____

_____

_____

_____

_____

29. Find the length of the midsegment of the trapezoid.

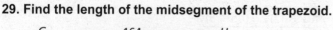

25. _____

26. _____

27. _____

28. _____

29. _____

30. _____

30. Find the value of *x* such that
$m\angle H = 8x°$ and $m\angle G = (10x - 38)°$
in the isosceles trapezoid.

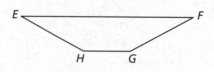

Name_____ Date _____

Chapter 7 Alternative Assessment

1. Draw a Venn diagram that shows the relationships among the special
   quadrilaterals you studied in Chapter 7. Show an example of each special
   quadrilateral in your Venn diagram with any relationships of its sides
   and angles labeled.

2. A faceted jewel is made by cutting the surface
   of a gemstone into flat, polygon-shaped faces
   called facets. The widest part of the gem, called
   the girdle, determines the outline shape of the gem.
   The top of a gem is the crown and the bottom is
   the pavilion. Some gems have a large, flat facet
   at the very top called the table.

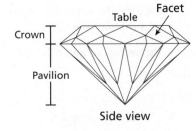

Side view

   a. The top view of a faceted gem is shown at the
      right. The table is a regular polygon. Find the
      measure of each interior angle of the table.

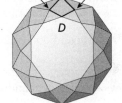

   b. Quadrilateral *ABCD* is a kite. State all the angles
      and sides of quadrilateral *ABCD* that are congruent.

   c. In the top view of a cross-rose cut gem shown at
      the right, all four sides of quadrilateral *EFGH* are
      congruent. List everything you know about this
      quadrilateral.

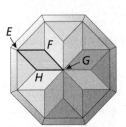

   d. In quadrilateral *EFGH*, $m\angle E = 49°$. Find
      $m\angle F$. Explain your reasoning.

   e. In the top view of the square gem shown to the
      right, $\overline{TW}$ is the midsegment of trapezoid *SUVX*,
      $\overline{SX}$ is the midsegment of trapezoid *RTWY*,
      $UV = 3$ millimeters, and $SX = 8$ millimeters.
      Find *TW*. Then find *RY*.

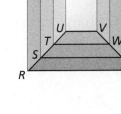

   f. You are checking the symmetry of a gemstone.
      A micrometer is a tool that measures length. How
      would you use a micrometer to show that that one
      of the facets of the gemstone is a parallelogram?

Chapter 7 Alternative Assessment Rubric

Score	Conceptual Understanding	Mathematical Skills	Work Habits
4	Shows complete understanding of: • Finding the angle measures of a regular polygon • Properties of quadrilaterals	Draws and labels a Venn diagram that correctly shows how all special quadrilaterals are related Uses the properties of polygons and quadrilaterals correctly in Exercise 2	Answers all parts of both problems The answers are correct and explained appropriately with mathematical terminology. Work is very neat and well organized.
3	Shows nearly complete understanding of: • Finding the angle measures of a regular polygon • Properties of quadrilaterals	Draws a Venn diagram that shows how most special quadrilaterals are related Uses most of the properties of polygons and quadrilaterals correctly in Exercise 2	Answers most parts of both problems Most of the answers are correct and explained with mathematical terminology. Work is neat and organized.
2	Shows some understanding of: • Finding the angle measures of a regular polygon • Properties of quadrilaterals	Draws a Venn diagram that shows some of the relationships of special quadrilaterals Fails to use the properties of polygons and quadrilaterals correctly in two or three parts of Exercise 2	Answers some parts of both problems Some of the answers are incorrect or incorrectly explained. Work is not very neat or organized.
1	Shows little understanding of: • Finding the angle measures of a regular polygon • Properties of quadrilaterals	Venn diagram is not drawn or fails to show many of the relationships of special quadrilaterals Fails to use the properties of polygons and quadrilaterals correctly in most parts of Exercise 2	Attempts few parts of either problem Most of the answers are incorrect, and the explanations are incorrect or not provided. Work is sloppy and disorganized.

Name_____ Date_____

Scissor Lifts

Instructional Overview	
Launch Question	A scissor lift is a work platform with an adjustable height that is stable and convenient. The platform is supported by crisscrossing beams that raise and lower the platform. What quadrilaterals do you see in the scissor lift design? What properties of those quadrilaterals play a key role in the successful operation of the lift?
Summary	Students measure components of a quadrilateral to prove that it is a parallelogram. Then using properties of parallelograms, they explain how a scissor lift elevates a platform while keep it parallel to the ground. The key here is that the shape of the parallelogram (in particular the rhombus) is preserved because the opposite sides remain congruent.
Teacher Notes	Students may want to state conclusions in this task without using the theorems because "it looks like it." The point of the task is to investigate *why* "it looks like it," so be ready to redirect students to the properties of parallelograms. Some students may classify the shape used in the lift as a parallelogram and not a rhombus. Encourage them to be as precise as possible with their language.
Supplies	Handout, protractors, rulers
Mathematical Discourse	Which geometric shapes add stability to objects? How?
Writing/Discussion Prompts	Identify another device or object that works under the same principles as the scissor lift. Explain.

Curriculum Content	
Content Objectives	• Use geometric shapes, their measures, and their properties to solve a design problem with given constraints.
Mathematical Practices	• Construct logical arguments to explain the operation of the lift. • Be precise in using terms, definitions, and theorems in logical arguments.

Chapter 7 **Performance Task** (continued)

Rubric

Scissor Lifts	Points
Students recognize properties of parallelograms. Students use theorems and definitions to justify their answers.	**22** Total possible points
1. *Sample answer:* rhombuses, triangles; Students should trace and label the shapes they see in the diagram.	**2** for each correct answer
2. rhombuses (this is more specific than parallelogram, which could also be accepted); All sides are congruent.	
3. parallel and congruent; Because a rhombus is a parallelogram, all sides are also parallel. Because it is a parallelogram, by the Parallelogram Opposite Sides Theorem (Theorem 7.3), its opposite sides are congruent.	
4. supplementary; In a parallelogram, consecutive interior angles are supplementary.	
5. increases by the same amount; By the Parallelogram Consecutive Angles Theorem (Theorem 7.5), if a quadrilateral is a parallelogram, then its consecutive angles are supplementary. Because supplementary angles must always sum to 180°, when one decreases, the other increases by the same amount.	
6. decreases by the same amount; By the Parallelogram Opposite Angles Theorem (Theorem 7.4), if a quadrilateral is a parallelogram, then its opposite angles are congruent.	
7. decreases by the same amount; By the Vertical Angles Congruence Theorem (Theorem 2.6), vertical angles are congruent.	
8. D, B, H, F, L, and J decrease while A, C, E, G, I, and K increase; All consecutive interior angle pairs must remain supplementary.	
9. They stay the same; The sides are only rotated, not dilated, so they remain congruent.	
10. The diagonals $\overline{DB}$, $\overline{HF}$, and $\overline{LJ}$ lengthen while others get shorter; Largest sides are opposite largest angles, so the lengths of the diagonals change with the angles.	
11. As the angles change, the shape of each quadrilateral remains a rhombus; While the vertical diagonals get longer, they remain perpendicular to the shorter diagonals and the sides remain parallel. So, the platform remains horizontal.	
Mathematics Practice: Students use definitions and theorems to explain what "looks" obvious. They specify "rhombus" as the key shape.	**3** For demonstration of practice; Partial credit can be awarded.
Total Points	**25 points**

Name_____ Date _____

Scissor Lifts

A scissor lift is a work platform with an adjustable height that is stable and convenient. The platform is supported by crisscrossing beams that raise and lower the platform. What quadrilaterals do you see in the scissor lift design? What properties of those quadrilaterals play a key role in the successful operation of the lift?

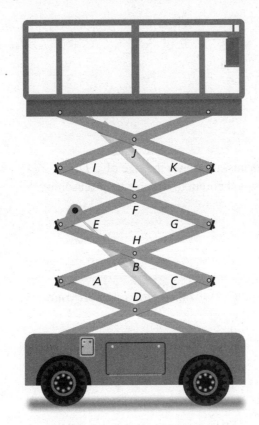

1. What geometric shapes do you see in the picture of a scissor lift? Trace and label them.

2. What special shape are the quadrilaterals *ABCD*, *EFGH*, and *IJKL*? How do you know this? Measure key components and use the theorems in this chapter to support your reasoning.

Chapter 7 **Performance Task** (continued)

3. What can you conclude about segments $\overline{AD}$ and $\overline{BC}$? $\overline{EH}$ and $\overline{FG}$? $\overline{IL}$ and $\overline{JK}$? Reference a theorem or definition to support your conclusion.

4. What is the relationship between $\angle A$ and $\angle D$? $\angle E$ and $\angle H$? $\angle I$ and $\angle L$? Explain.

5. For the scissor lift to operate, a mechanism changes the size of $\angle D$. As $\angle D$ decreases, what happens to $\angle A$? Use a theorem to support your reasoning.

6. As $\angle D$ decreases, what happens to $\angle B$? Use a theorem to support your reasoning.

7. As $\angle B$ decreases, what happens to $\angle H$? Use a theorem to support your reasoning.

8. Describe what happens to the rest of the angles in the scissor lift as $\angle D$ decreases. Explain your reasoning.

Performance Task (continued)

9. As the angles change size, what happens to the lengths of the sides of the quadrilateral? Explain your reasoning.

10. As the angles change size, what happens to the lengths of the diagonals of the quadrilateral? Explain your reasoning.

11. As the angles change size, what happens to the shape of the quadrilateral? Explain how this preserves the stability of the platform on the scissor lift.

Name_____ Date _____

List all pairs of congruent angles. Then write the ratios of the corresponding side lengths in a statement of proportionality.

Answers

1. $\triangle LNM \sim \triangle ABC$

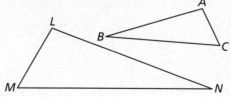

1. _____

_____

2. $DEFG \sim MNOP$

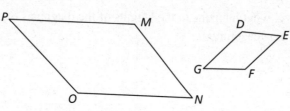

2. _____

_____

_____

The polygons are similar. Find the value of *x*.

3.

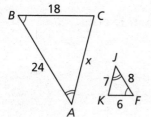

4.

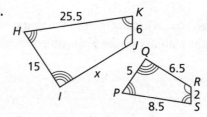

3. _____

4. _____

5. _____

6. _____

In the diagram *ABCD* ~ *WXYZ*. Find the ratio of their perimeters.

7. _____

5.

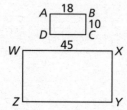

6.

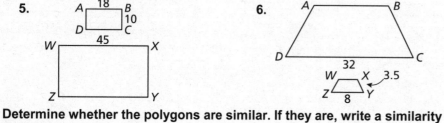

8. _____

9. _____

Determine whether the polygons are similar. If they are, write a similarity statement.

7.

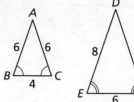

8.

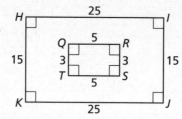

Show that the two triangles are similar.

10. _____

9.

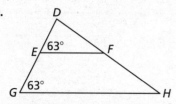

10.

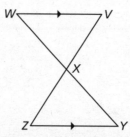

_____

_____

_____

_____

_____

_____

Name_____ Date_____

Chapter 8 Test A

Determine whether the polygons are similar.

Answers

1.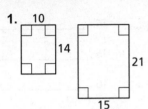
10
14
21
15

2.
7
5
21
15

3.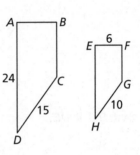
28
12.4 12.4
20
25
15.5 15.5
35

1. _____

2. _____

3. _____

4. _____

5. _____

6. _____

In the diagram, *ABCD ~ EFGH*. Find the following.

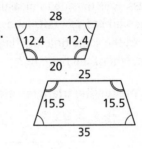

4. scale factor

5. *EH*

6. *AB*

7. _____

8. _____

9. _____

10. _____

11. _____

**In the diagram, *LMNO ~ PQRS*. Complete
the proportions and congruence statements.**

7. ∠*P* ≅ _____

8. ∠*M* ≅ _____

9. $\dfrac{MN}{RQ} = \dfrac{LM}{?}$

10. Find the value of *x*.

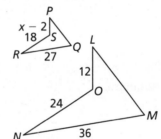

**Determine whether the triangles are similar. If they are, write a similarity
statement. Explain your reasoning.**

11.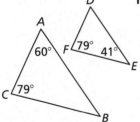
D
A
79°
60° F 41°
E
79°
C
B

12.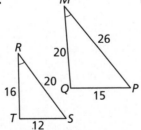
M
26
R
20
16 20 Q
P
15
T 12 S

13.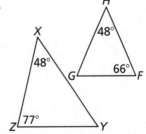
H
48°
X
48° G 66° F
77°
Z Y

12. _____

13. _____

14. Your geometry class goes outside to measure the height of the school's flagpole. A student who is 5 feet tall stands up straight and casts a shadow that is 8 feet long. At the same time the flagpole casts a shadow that is 24 feet long. What is the height of the flagpole?

Answers

14. _____

15. _____

16. _____

17. _____

18. _____

19. _____

20. _____

21. _____

22. _____

23. _____

24. _____

25. _____

26. _____

Find the value of x that makes the triangles similar.

15.
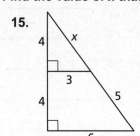

16.
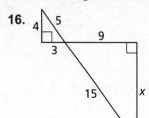

17.
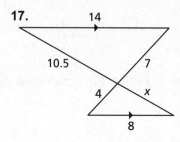

Find the value of x so that $\overline{BC} \parallel \overline{DE}$.

18.
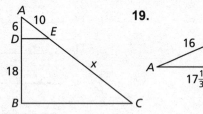

19. 20.
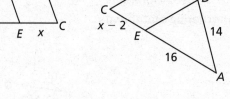

Determine the length of the segment.

21. $\overline{AG}$

22. $\overline{FC}$

23. $\overline{FE}$

24. $\overline{ED}$

25. $\overline{AE}$

26. $\overline{AD}$

Chapter 8 Test B

The given polygons are similar. Find the value of *x*.

Answers

1.
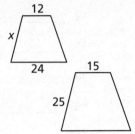

2.
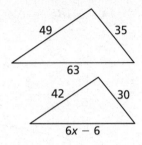

3.
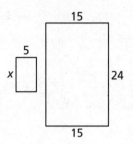

1. _____

2. _____

3. _____

4. _____

Find the scale factor. Then list all the pairs of congruent angles and write the ratios of the corresponding side lengths in a statement of proportionality.

4.
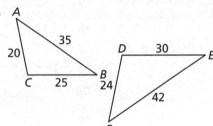

5.
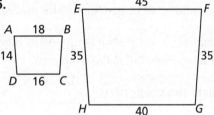

5. _____

6. _____

7. _____

8. _____

6. Pittsburgh, Pennsylvania and State College, Pennsylvania are 9.8 inches apart on a map that has a scale showing 1.1 inches equal to 15 miles. How far apart are the cities in real life?

7. A model house is 12 centimeters long. If it was built with a scale factor of 3 centimeters equal to 7 feet, then how long is the house in real life?

9. _____

Show that the triangles are similar. Write a similarity statement.

8.

9.
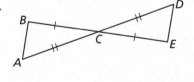

10. _____

Can the given information be used to prove △*ABC* ~ △*EDC*? Explain your reasoning.

10. $ED = 8$, $DC = 10$, $EC = 12$, $AB = 12$, $BC = 15$, $AC = 21$

11. $ED = 7$, $DC = 9$, $AB = 10.5$, $BC = 13.5$, $m\angle BAC + m\angle BCA = 105°$

11. _____

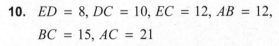
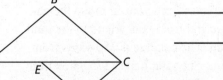

Chapter 8 **Test B** (continued)

The triangles in each pair are similar. Find the value of *x*.

12. △*DBC* ~ △*TRS*   **13.** △*ABC* ~ △*DEC*   **14.** △*ABE* ~ △*ACD*

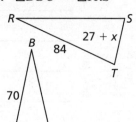

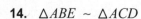

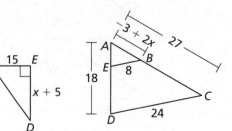

15. Your geometry class goes on a field trip to the zoo. If an 18-foot tall tree casts a 9 foot-long shadow, how tall is an adult giraffe that casts a 7-foot shadow?

16. A 4-foot tall girl stands 6.5 feet from a lamp post at night. Her shadow from the light is 2.5 feet long. How tall is the lamp post?

Use the figure to complete the proportion.

17. $\dfrac{EF}{FG} = \dfrac{BA}{?}$ **18.** $\dfrac{CB}{BA} = \dfrac{?}{EF}$

19. $\dfrac{AB}{AC} = \dfrac{?}{FD}$ **20.** $\dfrac{GF}{GD} = \dfrac{GA}{?}$

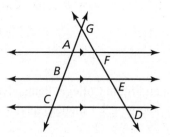

Answers

12. _____

13. _____

14. _____

15. _____

16. _____

17. _____

18. _____

19. _____

20. _____

21. _____

22. _____

23. _____

24. _____

Find the value of *x*.

21.   **22.**   **23.**

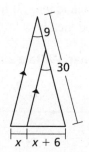

24. Your friend is hitting a golf ball toward the hole. The line from your friend to the hole bisects the angle formed by the lines from your friend to the oak tree and from your friend to the sand trap. The oak tree is 250 yards from him. The sand trap is 375 yards from him. The hole is 225 yards from the sand trap. How far is the hole from the oak tree?

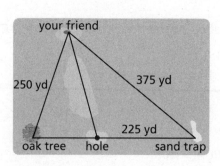

Name_____ Date_____

1. The figure shows the plans for a railing on a ramp.

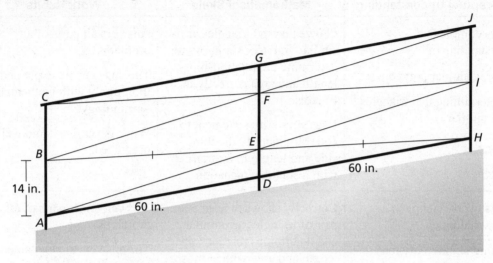

   a. Use the information in the figure to show that $\triangle ABH \sim \triangle DEH$.

   b. Find *DE*. Explain your reasoning

   c. Show that $\overline{AC} \parallel \overline{DG}$.

   d. Show that $\triangle ACI \sim \triangle EFI$.

   e. Given that quadrilateral *ABED* is similar to quadrilateral *ACIH*, and the approximate area of quadrilateral *ABED* is 617 square inches, find the approximate area of quadrilateral *ACIH*. Explain your reasoning.

   f. The top of the railing must be at least 32 inches above the ramp surface. Given that quadrilateral *ABED* is similar to quadrilateral *ACIH*, what vertical distance is needed between the ramp surface and $\overline{AH}$? Explain your reasoning.

2. Consider $\triangle XYZ$ shown below and $\triangle STU$ (not shown). Two sides of $\triangle STU$ have lengths of 15 feet and 30 feet, and $\triangle XYZ \sim \triangle STU$. Identify the third side of $\triangle STU$ and find its length. Explain your reasoning.

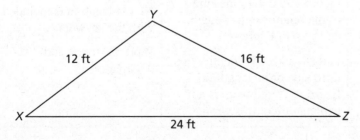

Chapter 8 Alternative Assessment Rubric

Score	Conceptual Understanding	Mathematical Skills	Work Habits
4	Shows complete understanding of: • Using similar polygons • Determining that triangles are similar	Shows that the triangles are similar and uses similarity to determine the relationships, length and area correctly in Exercise 1 Uses similarity statement to correctly identify the third side and length in Exercise 2, with a sound explanation	Answers all parts of all problems The answers are explained thoroughly with mathematical terminology. Work is very neat and well organized.
3	Shows nearly complete understanding of: • Using similar polygons • Determining that triangles are similar	Correctly shows at least one pair of triangles are similar and determines relationships, length and area with at most one error in Exercise 1 Uses similarity statement to correctly identify the third side and length in Exercise 2, but explanation may be incorrect or incomplete	Answers most parts of all problems The answers are explained with mathematical terminology. Work is neat and organized.
2	Shows some understanding of: • Using similar polygons • Determining that triangles are similar	Shows at most one pair of triangles similar and has more than one error in determining relationships, length and area in Exercise 1 May fail to correctly identify the third side or its length in Exercise 2, and explanation is incorrect or not provided	Answers some parts of all problems The answers are poorly or incorrectly explained. Work is not very neat or organized.
1	Shows little understanding of: • Using similar polygons • Determining that triangles are similar	Fails to show more than one pair of triangles similar and incorrectly determines most of the relationships, length, and area in Exercise 1 Fails to correctly identify the third side or its length in Exercise 2, and there is no explanation or it is wrong	Answers few parts of any problem No explanation is included with the answers. Work is sloppy and disorganized.

Name_____ Date _____

Performance Task

Judging the Math Fair

Instructional Overview	
Launch Question	You have been selected to be one of the judges for the Middle School Math Fair. In one competition, the sixth graders were asked to create similar figures of real-life models. As a judge, you need to verify that the objects are scaled correctly in at least two different ways. How will you document that the entries are correct?
Summary	The students are provided a drawing of a scale model wind generator as well as the dimensions of the real generator. After determining if the model is actually similar, the students are asked to create a rubric (scoring guide) to use for judging the math fair. The final component is for students to use the rubric to judge their work in the first problem.
Teacher Notes	The first problem is provided to help the students begin to think what would be necessary to decide if an object is similar. Remind students that when they are actually constructing an object, there should be a little room for error. Discuss what might be acceptable. Do they want to think about angles, circumference, height, or something else? The next step is to include at least two different mathematical criteria for judging the fair. Make sure the students have had some experience with scoring guides. The discussion prompts might be best used preceding the task. This is a task where students would benefit from working with a team to complete the rubric creation.
Supplies	Handouts, calculators
Mathematical Discourse	What are the criteria you would want considered if someone were judging your project? What is the definition of similar? Why should things besides just similarity be considered? How much error should be allowed in the sixth graders' work? Does it depend on the original size?
Writing/Discussion Prompts	1. Would you enjoy judging a math fair using your scoring guide? Why or why not? 2. Have you ever built a scale model? What do you think would be the hardest part?

Chapter 8 Performance Task (continued)

Judging the Math Fair

Curriculum Content	
Content Objectives	• Use congruence and similarity criteria to prove that a model of an object is similar to the object.
Mathematical Practices	• Use mathematics to model scale replicas of objects. • Be precise in measuring angles and lengths of objects and their scale models.

Rubric

Judging the Math Fair	Points	
1. The turbine picture is similar to the GE model; The student shows that the components have the same ratio and the angle measures are the same. The scale is 8 feet to 1 inch.	**6** **4** **2** **1**	There are at least two correct ratios shown, and two equal angle measures are mentioned. One correct ratio and a mention of equal angles Small errors in the work and angles are ignored A correct start
2. Students create a rubric with the required components. *Sample answer*:	**8** **6** **4** **2**	Meets all of criteria listed, mathematically accurate Meets most of the criteria and only a minor error Some criteria met with minor error A good start with a few relevant statements

Point Value	Criteria
6	Three angles within the object are accurate and correct within 3°.
6	Three different length measurements contain the same ratio to the nearest whole number.
2	The colors are similar to the original.
2	Creativity—The model is interesting to other students.
4	Appearance—The model looks like the real object.
20	Total Points

Performance Task (continued)

Rubric (continued)

	3.	
	Sample answer:	

Point Value	Criteria	Evaluation Explanation
6	Three angles within the object are accurate and correct within 3°.	The angles between the blades are all 120°, the angle between the base and column is 90°, and the angle between the column and motor is 90°. 6 points
6	Three different length measurements contain the same ratio to the nearest whole number.	The ratio of the length of the blades, the height of the tower, and total height of the windmill are all the same ratio. 6 points
2	The colors are similar to the original.	Both are white. 2 points
2	Creativity—The model is interesting to other students.	It is not very interesting. 1 point
4	Appearance—The model looks like the real object.	It looks similar, but the workmanship is a little rough. 3 points
20	Total Points	18

4 Evaluated accurately
2 Minor errors

Chapter 8 **Performance Task** (continued)

Rubric (continued)

4. *Sample answer:* A child's small chair

Point Value	Criteria	Evaluation Explanation
6	Three angles within the object are accurate and correct within 3°.	The angles between the base and back are the same, the angle between the seat and back is off by 5°, and the arm and back have the same angle. 4 points
6	Three different length measurements contain the same ratio to the nearest whole number.	The ratio of the arm lengths and width of seat are the same. The total height is off by more than 1 unit. 4 points
2	The colors are similar to the original.	The chairs have the same pattern and basic color. 2 points
2	Creativity—The model is interesting to other students.	The model is aesthetically pleasing and interesting to others. 2 points
4	Appearance—The model looks like the real object.	The model is well made with the same material. 4 points
20	Total Points	16

Mathematics Practice: Mathematical modeling demonstrated and vocabulary/mathematics are accurate	**3**	Students demonstrate an understanding of the role mathematics plays in accurate modeling. Partial credit can be awarded.
Total Points	**21 points**	

Name_____ Date _____

Judging the Math Fair

You have been selected to be one of the judges for the Middle School Math Fair.
In one competition, the sixth graders were asked to create similar figures of real-life
models. As a judge, you need to verify that the objects are all scaled correctly in at
least two different ways. How will you document the entries are correct?

1. Review the dimensions of a standard wind turbine made by General Electric.
   Is the turbine in the picture similar to the GE model? Explain why or why not.
   Use the information from this chapter to support your decision.

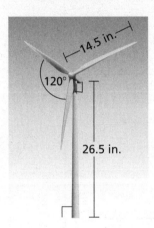

Specifications for the GE 1.5-megawatt Wind Turbine	
Blade Length	116 ft
Tower Height	212 ft
Total Height	328 ft
Angle Between Blades	120°

Name _____ Date _____

Judging the Math Fair

2. Create a 20-point scoring guide to judge the math fair projects. Your guide must include two different ways to check that the items are similar and that the students have created the model to accurate dimensions. At least 12 of your points need to be awarded for the mathematical components. Remember, it is difficult to be exact, so think about how much room you should allow for construction error. There must be at least five different components to your rubric.

Point Value	Criteria
20	Total Points

Name_____ Date_____

Chapter 8 Performance Task (continued)

Judging the Math Fair

3. Use the rubric you created to grade the wind turbine replica in Exercise 1. Explain your evaluation.

4. Select an item and measure its key components. Then draw a sketch of that item with attention to scale. Grade your drawing with the scoring guide you created. Include the key measurements of your real object and your scale drawing.

Chapter 9 Quiz
For use after Section 9.3

Find the value of *x*. Tell whether the side lengths form a Pythagorean triple.

Answers

1.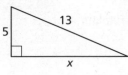

2.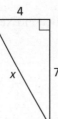

3.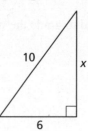

1. _____

_____

2. _____

_____

Find the area of the isosceles triangle.

4.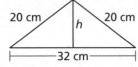

5.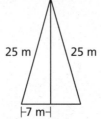

3. _____

_____

4. _____

5. _____

6. _____

Verify that the segment lengths form a triangle. Is the triangle *acute*, *right*, or *obtuse*?

7. _____

6. 9, 12, 17   **7.** 9.2, 15.1, 17.4   **8.** 24, 45, 51

8. _____

9. _____

Find the values of *x* and *y*. Write your answer in simplest form.

9.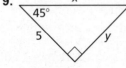

10.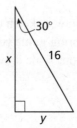

11.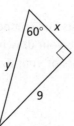

_____

10. _____

_____

_____

11. _____

_____

Find the geometric mean of the two numbers.

12. _____

12. 9 and 4   **13.** 6 and 96   **14.** 7 and 9

13. _____

14. _____

Identify the similar right triangles. Then find the value of the variable.

15.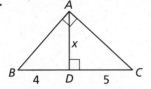

16.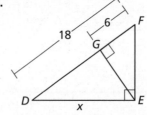

15. _____

_____

_____

_____

16. _____

_____

Name_____ Date_____

Find the value of x. Then tell whether the side lengths form a Pythagorean triple. *Answers*

1.

2.

3.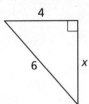

Do the following segment lengths form a triangle? If so, is the triangle *acute*, *obtuse*, or *right*?

4. 2, 4, 8   **5.** 5, 6, 7   **6.** 6, 8, 15   **7.** 9, 12, 15

8. A helicopter rose vertically 325 meters and then flew east 500 meters. How far is the helicopter from its starting point?

Find the values of x and y. Write your answer in simplest form.

9.

10.

11.

Identify the similar triangles. Then find the value of x.

12.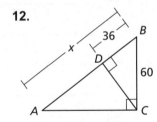

13.

14.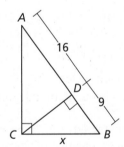

Find the geometric mean of the two numbers.

15. 15 and 20   **16.** 4 and 18   **17.** 3 and 12

Answers
1. _____
_____
2. _____
_____
3. _____
_____
4. _____
5. _____
6. _____
7. _____
8. _____
9. _____
_____
10. _____
_____
11. _____
_____
12. _____
_____
13. _____
_____
14. _____
_____
15. _____
16. _____
17. _____

Find tan *A* and tan *B*. Write each answer as a fraction and as a decimal rounded to the nearest hundredth.

Answers

18.

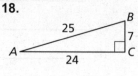

19.

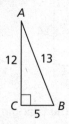

20.

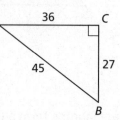

18. _____

_____

19. _____

_____

_____

20. _____

Find the value of *x*. Round your answer to the nearest tenth.

21.

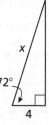

22.

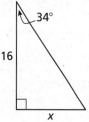

23.

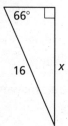

21. _____

22. _____

23. _____

24. _____

Use the diagram. Write your answer as a fraction and as a decimal rounded to the nearest hundredth.

24. sin *A*

25. cos *A*

26. sin *B*

27. cos *B*

25. _____

_____

26. _____

27. _____

_____

28. _____

29. _____

30. _____

28. A wheelchair ramp is 4.2 meters long. It rises up 0.7 meter. What is the angle of elevation to the nearest tenth of a degree?

29. You go to the park on a windy day to fly a kite. You have released 40 feet of string. The string makes an angle of 36° with the ground. How high is the kite in the air?

30. A 22-foot ladder is resting against the side of a building. The bottom of the ladder is 3 feet from the building. Find the measure of the angle the ladder makes with the ground. Round your answer to the nearest tenth of a degree.

Chapter 9 **Test B**

Find the value of x. Then tell whether the side lengths form a Pythagorean triple. *Answers*

1.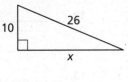

2.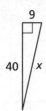

3.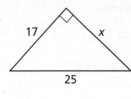

1. _____

_____

2. _____

4. You fly 470 miles due west from Chicago, Illinois, to Omaha, Nebraska. You then fly 437 miles to St. Louis, Missouri. Finally, you fly 300 miles back to Chicago. Is the triangle formed by your trip *acute*, *right*, or *obtuse*? Explain your reasoning.

3. _____

_____

4. _____

Find the value of x. Write your answer in simplest form.

5.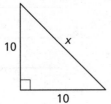

6.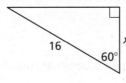

7.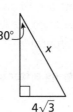

_____

_____

5. _____

6. _____

8. Your friend went on a trip to Kennywood Park. While there, he examined the inclined section of the roller-coaster track for the Phantom's Revenge. He noticed the ramp section rose at a 45° angle with the horizontal section, and connected at the top of the hill with a segment 100 feet long. These pieces formed a right angle at the top of the hill. Find *x*, the length from the point of inclination to the bottom of the hill.

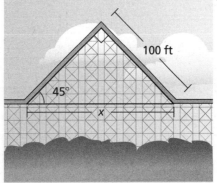

7. _____

8. _____

9. _____

10. _____

11. _____

_____

Find the values of x and y. Write your answer in simplest form.

9.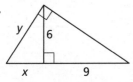

10.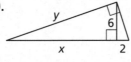

11.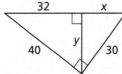

Name _____ Date _____

Find tan *A* and tan *B*. Write each answer as a fraction and as a decimal rounded to the nearest tenth.

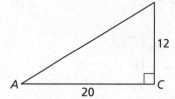

12. tan *A*   **13.** tan *B*

Find the measure of each angle to the nearest degree.

14. $m\angle A$ **15.** $m\angle B$

16. You look up at a 55° angle to see the top of a building. The vertical distance from the ground to your eye is 5.5 feet and the distance from you to the building is 57 feet. Estimate the height of the building.

17. A bird sits on top of a lamppost. The angle made by the lamppost and a line from the feet of the bird to the feet of an observer standing away from the lamppost is 55°. The distance from the lamppost to the observer is 25 feet. Estimate the height of the lamppost?

Use the figure. Write your answer as a fraction and as a decimal rounded to the nearest hundredth.

18. sin *A*   **19.** cos *A*

20. sin *B*   **21.** cos *B*

Find the values of *x* and *y*. Round your answer to the nearest tenth.

22. 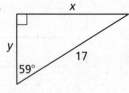   **23.** 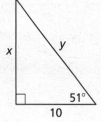   **24.**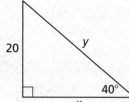

Answers

12. _____

_____

13. _____

_____

14. _____

15. _____

16. _____

17. _____

18. _____

_____

19. _____

_____

20. _____

_____

_____

21. _____

_____

22. _____

_____

23. _____

_____

24. _____

_____

Name_____ Date _____

1. Part of any good kitchen design is a convenient work triangle. The work triangle of a kitchen is formed by the three main work sites: the refrigerator, sink, and stove. The work triangle for one kitchen is shown below.

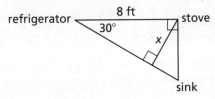

a. Find the distance between the stove and the sink. Explain your reasoning.

b. Determine whether the work triangle shown is *acute*, *right*, or *obtuse*. Explain.

c. Find the measure of the angle whose vertex is at the refrigerator. Round your answer to the nearest tenth.

The work triangle for a second kitchen is shown below.

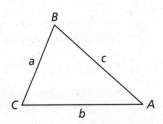

d. Find the distance from the stove to the sink. Round your answer to the nearest tenth.

e. Find the distance from the refrigerator to the sink. Round your answer to the nearest tenth.

f. Find the value of x.

g. Find the sine, cosine, and tangent of the angle whose vertex is at the sink.

h. Which design do you think is more convenient for heating up refrigerated leftovers on the stove? Which design do you think is more convenient for cleaning up after cooking? Explain your answers.

2. Explain how to find $m\angle A$ in $\triangle ABC$ under the given conditions.

a. You know the lengths of sides a, b, and c.

b. You know $m\angle B$, and the lengths of sides a and b.

Chapter 9 Alternative Assessment Rubric

Score	Conceptual Understanding	Mathematical Skills	Work Habits
4	Shows complete understanding of: • Solving right triangles • Applying the Law of Cosines and the Law of Sines	Correctly applies the Pythagorean Theorem (Theorem 9.1), the sine, cosine, and tangent ratios, and solving special and similar right triangles in Exercise 1 Correctly suggests using the Law of Cosines and the Law of Sines in Exercise 2	Answers all parts of all problems The answers are explained thoroughly with mathematical terminology. Work is very neat and well organized.
3	Shows nearly complete understanding of: • Solving right triangles • Applying the Law of Cosines and the Law of Sines	Applies the Pythagorean Theorem (Theorem 9.1), the sine, cosine, and tangent ratios, and solving special and similar right triangles in Exercise 1 with a few errors Suggests using the Law of Cosines and the Law of Sines in Exercise 2 Makes a total of one or two errors	Answers most parts of all problems The answers are explained with mathematical terminology. Work is neat and organized.
2	Shows some understanding of: • Solving right triangles • Applying the Law of Cosines and the Law of Sines	Fails to correctly apply the Pythagorean Theorem (Theorem 9.1), the sine, cosine, and tangent ratios, and solving special and similar right triangles in several parts of Exercise 1 Fails to suggest using the Law of Cosines or the Law of Sines in one or both parts of Exercise 2 Makes a total of up to five or six errors	Answers some parts of all problems The answers are poorly or incorrectly explained. Work is not very neat or organized.
1	Shows little understanding of: • Solving right triangles • Applying the Law of Cosines and the Law of Sines	Answers very little of Exercise 1 correctly Does not correctly suggest either the Law of Cosines or the Law of Sines in Exercise 2 Provides very few correct answers	Attempts few parts of any problem Little or no explanation is included with the answers. Work is sloppy and disorganized.

Chapter 9 **Performance Task**

Triathlon

Instructional Overview	
Launch Question	There is a big triathlon in town, and you are trying to take pictures of your friends at multiple locations during the event. How far would you need to walk to move between the photography locations?
Summary	The students will use triangles lengths, and angles to find the different lengths by applying the Pythagorean Theorem (Theorem 9.1), special right triangles, the Law of Cosines, or the Law of Sines.
Teacher Notes	For a triathlon, an Intermediate (or Standard) distance, commonly referred to as the "Olympic distance" includes swimming 1.5 kilometers (0.93 mile), biking 40 kilometers (25 miles), and running 10 kilometers (6.2 miles). This task involves an imaginary course with different distances labeled. Students will use the different theorems and skills learned in this chapter to calculate the distance the photographer would travel.
Supplies	Handout, calculator
Mathematical Discourse	Have you or someone you know ever completed in a triathlon? What are the three events involved in the triathlon? Why would someone taking pictures not want to travel the same route as the contenders?
Writing/Discussion Prompts	1. Which one of the distances was the most difficult to find? Why? 2. Are these lengths reasonable considering the typical triathlon distances? Support your answers.

Name_____ Date _____

Triathlon

Curriculum Content	
Content Objectives	• Use the Pythagorean Theorem. • Find a side length in 30°-60°-90° triangle. • Use the Law of Sines and the Law of Cosines.
Mathematical Practices	• Persevere in solving triangles by selecting the correct method to find the missing measure. • Model the path using triangles and use triangle theorems to find distances.

Rubric

Triathlon	Points
1. about 3.6 km; Right triangle (used Pythagorean Theorem, Theorem 9.1) with hypotenuse of $\sqrt{13} \approx 3.6$ 2. $\dfrac{8\sqrt{3}}{3} \approx 4.62$ km; special 30°-60°-90° triangle 3. about 6.78 km; Law of Sines $\dfrac{6 \cdot \sin(60°)}{\sin(50°)} \approx 6.78$ 4. about 7.36 km; Law of Sines $\dfrac{6 \cdot \sin(70°)}{\sin(50°)} \approx 7.36$ 5. about 10.66 km; Law of Cosines $6^2 + 7^2 - 2(6)(7)\cos(110°) \approx 10.66$	**15** Total possible points **3** For each problem: 1 for naming the method used, 1 for showing work, and 1 for listing the correct answer.
Mathematics Practice: Problem solving and use of mathematical structure are demonstrated throughout the activity.	**3** Students persevere to the end and use the structure of triangles to find the correct distances. Partial credit can be awarded.
Total Points	**18 points**

Name_____ Date_____

Performance Task (continued)

Triathlon

There is a big triathlon in town, and you are trying to take pictures of your friends at multiple locations during the event. How far would you need to walk to move between the photography locations?

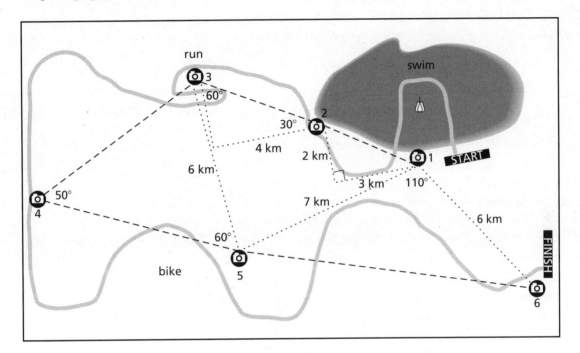

You are going to travel along the dashed path from Station 1 through Station 6. Use the information provided to find the distances between each photography spot. Name the theorem or property used and show how you found your answer.

Chapter 9 **Performance Task** (continued)

Triathlon

1. Station 1 to Station 2

2. Station 2 to Station 3

3. Station 3 to Station 4

Chapter 9 **Performance Task** (continued)

Triathlon

4. Station 4 to Station 5

5. Station 5 to Station 6

Name_____ Date _____

Chapters
7–9 **Cumulative Test**

1. The statements are given for a two-column proof. Provide a reason for each statement.

   Given   *ABCD* and *GDEF* are parallelograms.

   Prove $\angle A \cong G$

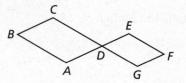

STATEMENTS	REASONS
1. *ABCD* and *GDEF* are parallelograms.	1.
2. $\angle CDA \cong \angle EDG$	2.
3. $m\angle CDA + m\angle A = 180°$	3.
4. $m\angle EDG + m\angle G = 180°$	4.
5. $m\angle CDA + m\angle A = m\angle EDG + m\angle G$	5.
6. $m\angle CDA = m\angle EDG$	6.
7. $m\angle CDA + m\angle A = m\angle CDA + m\angle G$	7.
8. $m\angle A = m\angle G$	8.
9. $\angle A \cong \angle G$	9.

2. Find the perimeter of polygon *ABCDEF*. Is the polygon equilateral? Equiangular? Regular? Explain your reasoning.

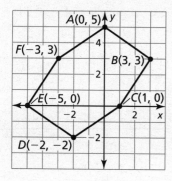

Chapters 7–9 **Cumulative Test** (continued)

3. Choose the correct symbols to complete the following proof.

Given △ABC

Prove △ABC can have at most one obtuse angle.

Indirect Proof

Step 1 Assume temporarily that △ABC has two obtuse angles, ∠A and ∠B. Then if follows that $m\angle A$ ____ 90° and $m\angle B$ ____ 90°.

Step 2 Given △ABC, $m\angle A + m\angle B + m\angle C$ ____ 180° by the Triangle Sum Theorem (Theorem 5.1).
If $m\angle A$ ____ 90° and $m\angle B$ ____ 90°, then $m\angle A + m\angle B + m\angle C$ ____ 180° by substitution.

Step 3 The conclusion contradicts the statement that $m\angle A + m\angle B + m\angle C$ ____ 180°. So, the temporary assumption that △ABC has two obtuse angles cannot be true. This proves that △ABC can have at most one obtuse angle.

| > | < | = | ≠ | ≅ |

4. Use the Rectangle Diagonals Theorem (Theorem 7.13) to prove that △ACE is an isosceles triangle.

Given ABCD is a rectangle and BCED is a parallelogram.

Prove △ACE is an isosceles triangle.

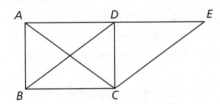

Cumulative Test (continued)

5. Use the graph of quadrilaterals *JKLM* and *PQRS*.

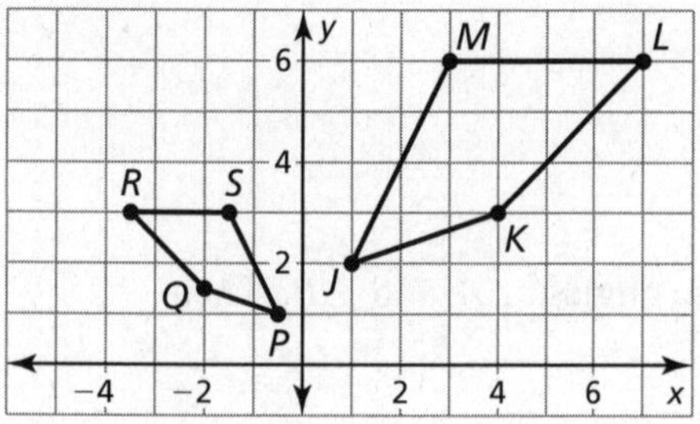

a. Write a composition of transformations that maps quadrilateral *JKLM* to quadrilateral *PQRS*.

b. Are the quadrilaterals similar? Explain your reasoning.

6. In the diagram of *ABCD*, which congruence theorem(s) could you use to show that $\triangle AED \cong \triangle AEB$?

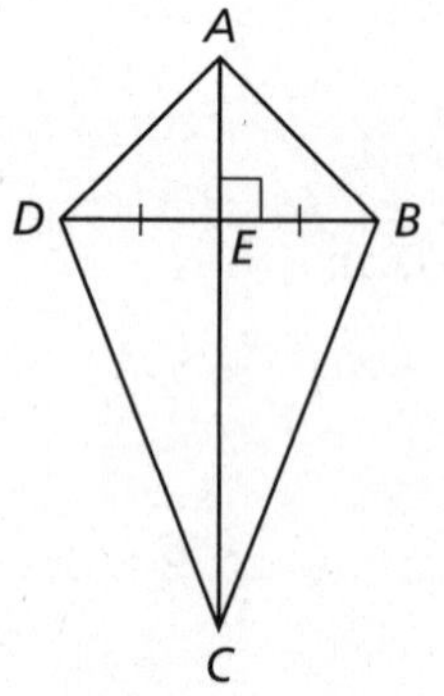

SAS Congruence Theorem (Theorem 5.5)

SSS Congruence Theorem (Theorem 5.8)

HL Congruence Theorem (Theorem 5.9)

ASA Congruence Theorem (Theorem 5.10)

AAS Congruence Theorem (Theorem 5.11)

7. By the Triangle Angle-Bisector Theorem (Theorem 8.9), $\frac{BC}{CD} = \frac{AB}{AD}$. In the diagram, $BC < AB$ and $CD < AD$. Find three possible values for *BC* and *CD*.

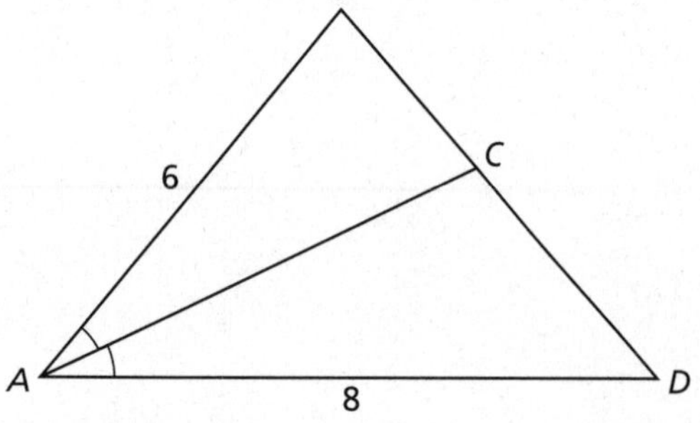

Name_____ Date_____

8. The slope of line p is $\frac{1}{5}$. The slope of line q is $\frac{1}{5}$. What *cannot* be true about lines p and q? Choose all that apply.

    A. Lines p and q are parallel.   **B.** Lines p and q are perpendicular.

    C. Lines p and q are skew.   **D.** Lines p and q are the same line.

9. The coordinates of the vertices of $\triangle ABC$ are $A(-12, 3)$, $B(-9, 6)$, and $C(6, 9)$. The coordinates of the vertices of $\triangle JKL$ are $J(4, -1)$, $K(3, -2)$, and $L(-2, -3)$.

    $\angle B \cong \angle K$. Can you show that the ratio of the perimeters of $\triangle ABC$ and $\triangle JKL$ is equal to the ratios of their corresponding sides by using the Perimeters of Similar Polygons Theorem (Theorem 8.1)? If so, do so by listing the ratio of the perimeters and the ratios of the corresponding sides and writing a similarity transformation that maps $\triangle ABC$ to $\triangle JKL$. If not, explain why not.

10. Classify the quadrilateral using the most specific name.

    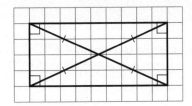

rectangle	square	parallelogram	rhombus

11. Your friend claims that quadrilateral *DEFG* is similar to quadrilateral *TUVW*. Describe the relationship between corresponding sides and the areas of the quadrilaterals that makes this statement true.

Chapters 7–9 **Cumulative Test** (continued)

12. You are considering four different sets of dimensions for a flower garden that is in the shape of a right triangle. You want a flower garden with the largest perimeter possible. Which dimensions should you choose?

A.
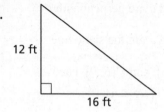
12 ft
16 ft

B.
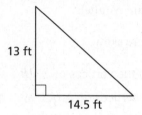
13 ft
14.5 ft

C.
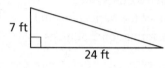
7 ft
24 ft

D.
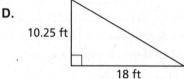
10.25 ft
18 ft

13. In △JKL, M is between K and L, and $JM^2 = KM \cdot LM$. What must be true about ∠J? Select all that apply.

| $m\angle J = 30°$ | $m\angle J = 45°$ | $m\angle J = 60°$ | $m\angle J = 90°$ |

14. In the diagram, △ABC ~ △DEF. Choose the symbol that makes each statement true.

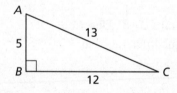
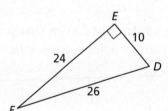

sin A ☐ sin F   sin A ☐ cos C   cos C ☐ cos F

tan C ☐ tan D   cos D ☐ cos F   sin C ☐ sin F

| < | = | > |

15. You are playing catch with your brother and your sister. You are represented by vertex A, your brother is represented by vertex B, and your sister is represented by vertex C. What is the distance between you and your brother? Round your answer to the nearest inch.

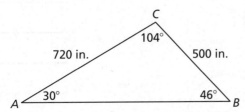

16. Create ten true equations about $\triangle PQR$, using only the boxes below.

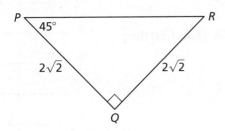

sin P	cos P	tan P
sin R	cos R	tan R

$\dfrac{PQ}{PR}$	$\dfrac{PQ}{QR}$	1
$\dfrac{QR}{PQ}$	$\dfrac{QR}{PR}$	$\dfrac{\sqrt{2}}{2}$

17. What are the coordinates of the vertices of the image of $\triangle UVW$ after the composition of transformations shown?

Translation: $(x, y) \rightarrow (x - 4, y + 1)$

Rotation: 90° about the origin

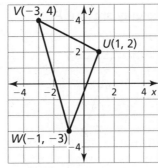

A. $U'(-3, 3), V'(-7, 5), W'(-5, -2)$

B. $U'(3, -3), V'(5, 7), W'(-2, 5)$

C. $U'(-3, -3), V'(-5, -7), W'(2, -5)$

D. $U'(3, -3), V'(7, -5), W'(5, 2)$

Name _____ Date _____

Chapter 10

Quiz

For use after Section 10.3

Use the diagram.

1. Name the circle. 2. Name a diameter.

3. Name a radius. 4. Name a secant.

5. Name a chord. 6. Name a tangent.

Find the value of *x*.

7.

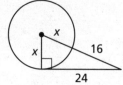

8.

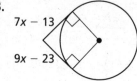

Identify the given arc as a *major arc*, *minor arc*, or *semicircle*. Then find the measure of the arc.

9. $\overset{\frown}{BC}$ 10. $\overset{\frown}{DBE}$

11. $\overset{\frown}{AED}$ 12. $\overset{\frown}{DE}$

Tell whether the gray arcs are congruent. Explain why or why not.

13.

14.

Find the measure of the gray arc in ⊙*P*.

15.

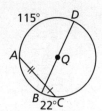

Answers

1. _____

2. _____

3. _____

4. _____

5. _____

6. _____

7. _____

8. _____

9. _____

   _____

10. _____

   _____

11. _____

   _____

12. _____

   _____

13. _____

   _____

14. _____

   _____

15. _____

Name_____ Date_____

Identify the line or segment as a *radius*, *chord*, *diameter*, *secant*, or *tangent* of ⊙L.

Answers

1. $\overline{KM}$ 2. $\overline{LN}$

3. $\overrightarrow{PM}$ 4. line n

5. $\overline{LQ}$ 6. $\overline{KN}$

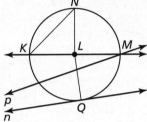

1. _____

2. _____

3. _____

4. _____

5. _____

6. _____

Points *K* and *L* are points of tangency. Find the value of *x*.

7.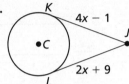

8.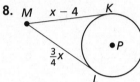

9.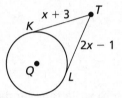

7. _____

8. _____

9. _____

10. Determine whether $\overline{FG}$ is tangent to ⊙E. Explain.

10. _____

_____

_____

_____

_____

Find the indicated measure.

11. $m\overarc{DEF}$ 12. $m\overarc{JKL}$ 13. $m\overarc{NGH}$

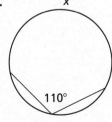

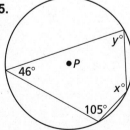

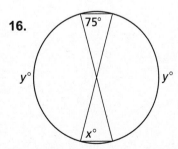

11. _____

12. _____

13. _____

14. _____

15. _____

Find the value of the variable(s).

14.   15.   16.

16. _____

_____

_____

Name _____ Date _____

Find the measure of the indicated line segment.

Answers

17. $\overline{UW}$

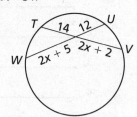

18. $\overline{NM}$

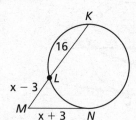

19. $\overline{KM}$

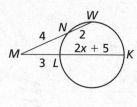

17. _____

18. _____

19. _____

20. _____

_____

Identify the center and the radius of the circle.

21. _____

20. $(x - 1)^2 + (y + 3)^2 = 4$ **21.** $(x - 2)^2 + (y - 1)^2 = 16$

_____

22. $x^2 + (y - 3)^2 = 14$ **23.** $(x - 1)^2 + (y + 4)^2 = 9$

22. _____

Use the given information to write the standard equation of the circle.

_____

24. a circle with center $(1, 2)$ and radius 5

23. _____

25. a circle with center $(-3, 5)$ and radius 2

_____

24. _____

26. Write the standard equation of a circle that is tangent to the *x*-axis, with the center located at $(2, 4)$.

25. _____

26. _____

27. Write the standard equation of a circle with the center at $(-1, -4)$ that passes through the point $(-1, -1)$.

27. _____

Name_____ Date_____

Use the diagram.

1. Name the diameter of ⊙G. **2.** Name a chord of ⊙F.

3. Name a common tangent.

4. Name a radius of ⊙F.

5. Name a point of tangency.

6. Name a secant.

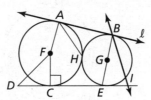

Answers

1. _____

2. _____

3. _____

4. _____

5. _____

6. _____

7. _____

8. _____

9. _____

10. _____

11. _____

12. _____

13. _____

14. _____

_____

15. _____

16. _____

17. _____

Points S and T are points of tangency. Find the value of x.

7.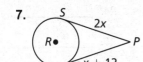

8.

9.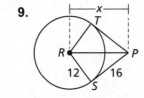

10. A belt is stretched between two pulleys, as shown. Find the approximate straight-line distance between W and X. Round your answer to the nearest tenth.

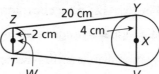

11. You are standing 25 feet from a water tower. The distance from you to the point of tangency on the tower is 45 feet. What is the radius of the water tower?

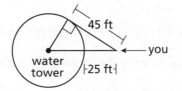

Find the indicated measure.

12. Find the value of x.   **13.** $m\overset{\frown}{BCD}$

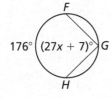

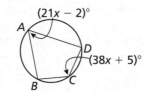

14. Find the values of x and y.

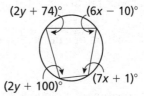

Find the value of x.

15.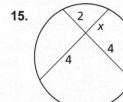

16.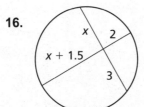

17.

Chapter 10 **Test B** (continued)

Find the indicated measure.

18. Find the value of *x*.

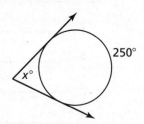

19. *m∠ABE*

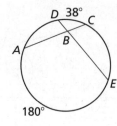

20. If line *m* is tangent to ⊙*Q*, find *mRST*.

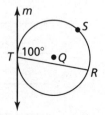

A radio tower is centered at (6, −12) on a coordinate grid where each unit represents 1 mile. The radio signal's range is 80 miles.

21. Write the standard equation that describes the position and range of the tower.

22. If you are located at the point (6, 75), would you receive the radio signal?

23. If you are located at the origin, would you receive the radio signal?

Use the given information to write the standard equation of the circle.

24. a circle with center (−5, 4) and radius 2

25. a circle with center (10, −2) and radius 6

26. The ends of the diameter fall at (18, −13) and (4, −3).

27. Write the standard equation of a circle that is tangent to the *y*-axis, with the center located at (−4, 6).

28. Write the standard equation of a circle with the center at (6, 8) that passes through the point (−1, 4).

Answers

18. _____

19. _____

20. _____

21. _____

22. _____

23. _____

24. _____

25. _____

26. _____

27. _____

28. _____

Chapter 10 **Alternative Assessment**

1. Explain how angles formed inside, outside, and on circles are related to arcs of the circles.

2. A circus ring is the arena where much of the action takes place at a circus. The figure below shows a circus ring with center O. $\overset{\frown}{AB}$ and $\overset{\frown}{DE}$ are openings in the circle to enter and exit the ring.

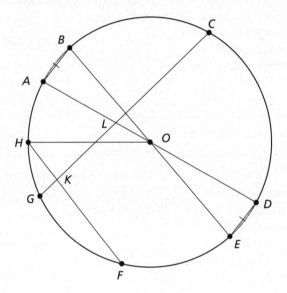

   a. Identify each segment in the figure as a *chord*, *diameter*, *radius*, or *tangent*.

   b. Given that $m\angle EOH = 131°$, find $m\overset{\frown}{EFH}$ and $m\overset{\frown}{ECH}$.

   c. The distances AB and DE are equal and $m\angle AOB = 20°$. Find $m\overset{\frown}{DE}$.

   d. Given that $m\overset{\frown}{ABC} = 90°$ and $m\overset{\frown}{GFD} = 126°$, find $m\angle GLD$.

   e. Let $HK = x + 4$, $FK = x + 14$, $GK = x$, and $CK = x + 32$. Find CG and FH.

   f. You are using a sheet of graph paper to plot a graph of the circus ring shown in the figure above. You draw a set of axes and place the center of the ring at the origin. Your circle has a radius of 21 units. Will the point $(14, 17)$ be on the circumference of the ring? Explain your reasoning.

Name _____ Date _____

Chapter 10 · Alternative Assessment Rubric

Score	Conceptual Understanding	Mathematical Skills	Work Habits
4	Shows complete understanding of: • Using properties of segments that intersect circles • Applying angle relationships in circles • Using circles in the coordinate plane	Gives correct and thorough explanations for all three cases in Exercise 1 Identifies segments, uses relationships of angles, arcs and segments of circles, and applies the equation of a circle correctly in Exercise 2	Answers all parts of all problems The answers are explained thoroughly with mathematical terminology. Work is very neat and well organized.
3	Shows nearly complete understanding of: • Using properties of segments that intersect circles • Applying angle relationships in circles • Using circles in the coordinate plane	Gives correct and thorough explanations for at least two of the cases in Exercise 1 Identifies segments, uses relationships of angles, arcs and segments of circles, and applies the equation of a circle with at most two errors in Exercise 2	Answers most parts of all problems The answers are explained with mathematical terminology. Work is neat and organized.
2	Shows some understanding of: • Using properties of segments that intersect circles • Applying angle relationships in circles • Using circles in the coordinate plane	Gives at least one correct explanation for in Exercise 1 Makes several errors identifying segments, using relationships of angles, arcs and segments of circles, and applying the equation of a circle in Exercise 2	Answers some parts of most problems The answers are poorly or incorrectly explained. Work is not very neat or organized.
1	Shows little understanding of: • Using properties of segments that intersect circles • Applying angle relationships in circles • Using circles in the coordinate plane	Gives at most one correct explanation in Exercise 1 Fails to attempt or makes errors on most parts of identifying segments, using relationships of angles, arcs and segments of circles, and applying the equation of a circle in Exercise 2	Attempts few parts of any problem No explanation is included with the answers. Work is sloppy and disorganized.

Chapter 10 Performance Task

Circular Motion

Instructional Overview	
Launch Question	What do properties of tangents tell us about the forces acting on a satellite orbiting around Earth? How would the path of the satellite change if the force of gravity were removed?
Summary	Students use the fact that the radius of a circle is perpendicular to a tangent of the circle at the endpoint of the radius to understand circular motion.
Teacher Notes	Students may struggle with the fact that in circular motion, velocity is actually perpendicular to acceleration. They may assume that it is opposite to the inward force of acceleration. When they spin on a merry-go-round, they "feel" that they are being pulled outward away from the merry-go-round instead of forward, tangent to the merry-go-round. It is easier for them to understand this with an example like a satellite orbiting Earth or a rock spinning in a sling. The perpendicular relationship is the reason that the rock will fly toward or the satellite will spin into space when the acceleration force is removed.
Supplies	Handout
Mathematical Discourse	What images come to mind when you hear the word "perpendicular"? Why is a satellite in orbit not one of those images?
Writing/Discussion Prompts	What other examples of circular motion can you think of?

Performance Task (continued)

Circular Motion

Curriculum Content	
Content Objectives	• Identify radii and tangents that intersect circles.
Mathematical Practices	• Model acceleration and velocity as radii and tangent of circles.

Rubric

Circular Motion	Points	
Students recognize that the path of an object in circular motion will always be tangent to the circular path when the inward force is removed. In Exercises 1–4, the path of the object is straight forward in a line that is tangent to its original circular path.	8	2 points for each problem answered correctly
Mathematics Practice: Model with mathematics. Students refer to the application when describing the path.	2	For demonstration of practice; Partial credit can be awarded.
Total Points	**10 points**	

Name_____ Date _____

Circular Motion

What do the properties of tangents tell us about the forces acting on a satellite orbiting around Earth? How would the path of the satellite change if the force of gravity were removed?

A satellite orbiting Earth is an example of an object in uniform circular motion. In this type of motion, an object travels around the perimeter of a circle at a constant speed as an acceleration force pulls it toward the center of the circle. For the satellite, this acceleration is the force of gravity.

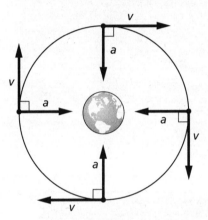

The key to the circular path is the relationship between the acceleration and the velocity of the object, which is the speed and direction it is moving. In this case, the force of the acceleration acts like the radius of the circle. To maintain a circular path, the velocity and acceleration must be perpendicular. This means that the velocity of an object in circular motion is tangent to its circular path, just as the Tangent Line to Circle Theorem (Theorem 10.1) describes the relationship between a line perpendicular to the endpoint of a radius of a circle.

If the inward force of acceleration is removed, the object will continue to move in the direction of its velocity. It will fly off in a straight line that is tangent to its circular path.

Using what you know about circles, tangents, and circular motion, describe the path of the following objects.

Chapter 10 Performance Task (continued)

1. To build momentum, an athlete spins 1.5 times through a circle before throwing a discus. The inward force on the discus points toward the body of the athlete. Describe the path of the discus as the athlete releases it.

Mark Herreid/Shutterstock.com

2. You attach a ball to a string and swing it in a horizontal circle. The tension of the string points inward toward your hand as you spin it. Describe the path of the ball if the string breaks.

Peter Baxter/Shutterstock.com

Chapter 10 Performance Task (continued)

3. You ride a spinning merry-go-round and hold tightly to the bar. The spinning causes a force on your body that points inward toward the center of the merry-go-round. Describe the path of your body if you release your grip.

Chepko Danil Vitalevich/Shutterstock.com

4. A skateboarder rides around the lip of a round bowl. The circular path creates a force on the boarder and board that points toward the center of the bowl. Describe the path of the skateboard if the wheels slip completely above the lip of the bowl and the boarder does not change his or her direction.

cdrin/Shutterstock.com

Name_____ Date _____

Find the indicated measure.

Answers

1. $m\overset{\frown}{DF}$

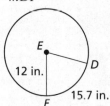

12 in.
15.7 in.

2. arc length of $\overset{\frown}{XZ}$

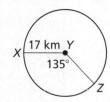

17 km Y
135°

3. circumference of $\odot C$

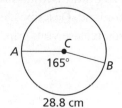

165°
28.8 cm

1. _____

2. _____

3. _____

4. _____

5. _____

6. _____

Convert degrees to radians and radians to degrees.

4. 240°

5. $\dfrac{13\pi}{18}$

7. _____

8. _____

Find the area of the shaded sector. Round your answer to the nearest tenth.

9. _____

6.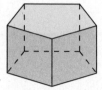

X 6 cm O
45°
Y

7.

F 240°
O
7 in.
E

10. _____

11. _____

12. _____

In the diagram, *ABCDEF* is a regular hexagon inscribed in circle $\odot O$.

8. Name the center.

9. Name a radius.

10. Name an apothem.

11. Name a central angle.

12. Find $m\angle BOA$, $m\angle AOP$, and $m\angle PAO$.

13. The radius of the circle is 8 units. Find the
area of the hexagon.

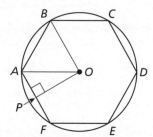

13. _____

14. _____

15. _____

16. _____

Tell whether the solid is a polyhedron. If it is, name the polyhedron.

14.

15.

16.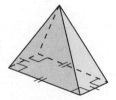

Chapter 11 Test A

Find the indicated measure.

Answers

1. circumference of ⊙R

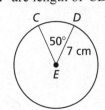

2. arc length of $\overarc{CD}$

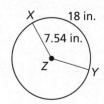

3. $m\overarc{XY}$

1. _____

2. _____

3. _____

4. _____

5. _____

Convert from degrees to radians.

4. 60°   **5.** 340°   **6.** −180°

6. _____

7. _____

Convert from radians to degrees.

7. $\dfrac{23\pi}{12}$ **8.** $\dfrac{10\pi}{6}$ **9.** $\dfrac{13\pi}{12}$

8. _____

9. _____

Find the area of the shaded region.

10. _____

10.

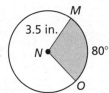

11.

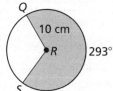

12.

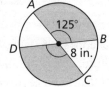

11. _____

12. _____

13. _____

14. _____

15. _____

13.

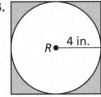

14.

15.

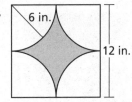

16. _____

16. Your friend is planting a circular garden full of different color pansies. Your friend plans to plant five different colors of equal amounts. The garden has a radius of 15 feet. How many square feet of space will each color cover?

Chapter 11 **Test A** (continued)

Find the area of the polygon.

Answers

17. kite

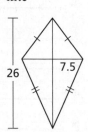

26   7.5

18. regular pentagon

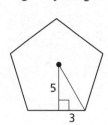

5

3

19. regular decagon

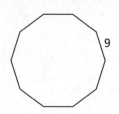

9

17. _____

18. _____

19. _____

20. _____

21. _____

22. _____

23. _____

24. _____

25. _____

Find the volume of the solid.

20.

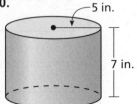

5 in.

7 in.

21.

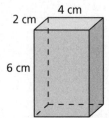

2 cm   4 cm

6 cm

22.

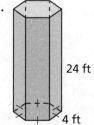

24 ft

4 ft

23. The Great Pyramid of Cheops is the largest pyramid in the world. It was built around 2500 B.C. by Khufu, or Cheops, a king of ancient Egypt. The pyramid has a square base of 230 meters on each side, and a height of 147 meters. Find the volume.

An official men's basketball has a diameter of 9.55 inches. The diameter of a women's basketball is 9.23 inches.

24. Find the difference of the volumes.

25. Find the difference of the surface areas.

Name_____ Date_____

1. A Ferris wheel has 18 seats. Passengers are let off one seat at a time, and then the wheel revolves until the next seat is on the platform. Each time a passenger is let off, each seat moves 20° and has an arc length of 10.5 feet. How far does each seat travel to make a complete revolution around the Ferris wheel?

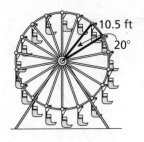

Answers

1. _____

2. _____

3. _____

4. _____

5. _____

6. _____

7. _____

8. _____

9. _____

10. _____

11. _____

12. _____

13. _____

14. _____

15. _____

2. A 20-inch diameter bicycle tire rotates 200 times. How many feet does the bicycle travel? Round your answer to the nearest foot.

3. A central angle of 62° intercepts an arc length of 90 units. What is the radius of the circle? Round your answer to the nearest hundredth.

4. A circle has a radius of 4 units. Find the measure of the central angle to the nearest tenth of a degree that intercepts an arc length of 5.8 units?

Convert degrees to radians and radians to degrees.

5. $-45°$

6. $\dfrac{3\pi}{5}$

7. $260°$

Find the area of the shaded region.

8.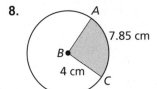

9.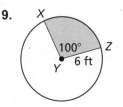

10.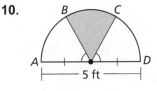

Find the area of the kite or rhombus.

11.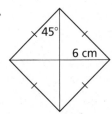

12.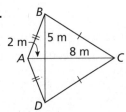

13.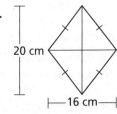

14. The area of a kite is 60 square meters. The length of one diagonal is 20 meters. What is the length of the other diagonal?

15. The area of a rhombus is 96 square inches. The length of a side is 10 inches and one of the diagonals measures 16 inches. What is the length of the other diagonal?

Find the area of the regular polygon.

16.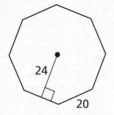

17.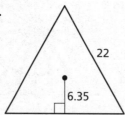

18.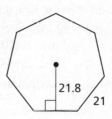

Answers

16. _____

17. _____

18. _____

19. ___See left.___

20. ___See left.___

21. _____

22. _____

23. _____

24. _____

Sketch the solid produced by rotating the figure around the given axis. Then identify and describe the solid.

19.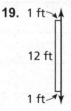

20.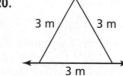

21. Your friend wants to donate clothes to a local shelter. He needs to choose the box that will hold the most clothes. Which box should he select? Explain your reasoning.

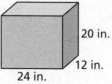

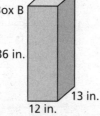

22. The Pyramid Arena was originally built as a 20,142 seat arena in downtown Memphis on the banks of the Mississippi River. It is 321 feet tall and has base sides of 591 feet. Find the volume of this structure.

23. How much ice cream can the sugar cone hold if you only fill the inside? Round your answer to the nearest cubic millimeter.

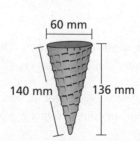

24. What is the surface area of the sugar cone? Round your answer to the nearest square centimeter. (Hint: The top of the cone is open and not included in the surface area.)

Chapter 11 Alternative Assessment

1. A home décor store sells products packaged in cardboard containers.

    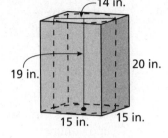

    a. A cylindrical drum is packaged in the rectangular prism-shaped box shown. Find the volume of the drum and the volume of the box.

    b. A triangular hole in the top of the box exposes a sector of the drum head with an intercepted arc of $\frac{\pi}{4}$ radian. What area of the drum head is exposed? Explain.

    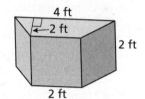

    c. A coffee table is packaged in the trapezoidal-prism shaped box shown. Find the volume of the box.

    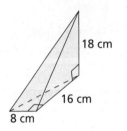

    d. A store sells the glass, pyramid-shaped bookend shown. Find the volume of the bookend. Does the figure give enough information to find the surface area of the bookend? Explain.

    e. The figure shows a cone-shaped candle packaged in a similar cone-shaped box. The cones have a scale factor of 3 : 5, and the volume of the box is 4909 cubic centimeters. Find the volume of the candle. Round your answer to the nearest cubic centimeter.

    f. The diameter of the circular base of the candle is 15 centimeters. Find the lateral surface area of the candle. Round your answer to the nearest tenth.

    g. A sphere-shaped globe is packaged in the regular hexagonal prism-shaped box shown. What is the area of each hexagonal base of the box? Explain how you found your answer.

    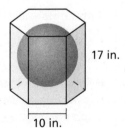

    h. The globe has a diameter of 16 inches. What volume of packing material is needed to fill the space in the box not taken up by the globe? Round your answer to the nearest cubic inch.

Chapter 11 Alternative Assessment Rubric

Score	Conceptual Understanding	Mathematical Skills	Work Habits
4	Shows complete understanding of: • Using radians and arc lengths • Solving problems involving surface area and volume • Using similarity of solids	Uses radian measure correctly Finds the volumes of the prisms, cylinder, pyramid, cones, and sphere Finds the areas of the sector, regular hexagon, and lateral surface of a cone All answers are complete and correct.	Answers all parts of the problem The answers are explained thoroughly with mathematical terminology. Work is very neat and well organized.
3	Shows nearly complete understanding of: • Using radians and arc lengths • Solving problems involving surface area and volume • Using similarity of solids	Uses radian measure correctly Finds the volumes of the prisms, cylinder, pyramid, cones, and sphere Finds the areas of the sector, regular hexagon, and lateral surface of a cone One or two answers are incomplete or incorrect.	Answers most parts of the problem The answers are explained with mathematical terminology. Work is neat and organized.
2	Shows some understanding of: • Using radians and arc lengths • Solving problems involving surface area and volume • Using similarity of solids	May not use radian measure correctly Finds at least four of the volumes and areas correctly	Answers some parts of the problem Many answers are poorly or incorrectly explained. Work is not very neat or organized.
1	Shows little understanding of: • Using radians and arc lengths • Solving problems involving surface area and volume • Using similarity of solids	May not use radian measure correctly Finds fewer than four of the volumes and areas correctly	Attempts few parts of any problem No explanation is included with the answers. Work is sloppy and disorganized.

Name_____ Date_____

 Performance Task

Waterpark Renovation

Instructional Overview	
Launch Question	The city council will consider reopening the closed water park if your team can come up with a cost analysis for painting some of the structures, filling the pool water reservoirs, and resurfacing some of the surfaces. What is your plan to convince the city council to open the water park?
Summary	The students will be able to compute the cost of two parts of the renovations and then add their cost to the group expenses. The final step allows students to add their costs and explain why they think the park should reopen.
Teacher Notes	The students could research materials and work with the numbers they find in their area. A roofing square is a square yard. The proposal for making money can go in many directions.
Supplies	Copies of handout, calculators
Mathematical Discourse	Discuss the different expenses associated with running a waterpark and a reasonable admission cost. Make sure students know that most financial problems are not solved over one year.
Writing/Discussion Prompts	1. How much of the admission costs do you think water and amusement parks save for improvements? Explain. 2. What percentages of the admission do you believe should be devoted to operational costs, future improvements, and income?

Curriculum Content	
Content Objectives	• Use the formulas for circumference to find measures in circles. • Find areas of polygons. • Find and use volumes of cylinders.
Mathematical Practices	• Construct a viable argument for reopening the water park. • Model features of the waterpark using geometric shapes.

Chapter 11 **Performance Task** (continued)

Rubric

Waterpark Renovation	Points
1. a. $(90^2 - 85^2)\pi = 875\pi$ ft^2, $875\pi \cdot 4 = 3500\pi$ ft^3; $3500\pi \cdot 7.48 \approx 82{,}247$ gal **b.** paint shed: $150 + 150 + 200 + 200 = 700$ ft^2; roof triangles: $2 \cdot \frac{1}{2} \cdot 20 \cdot 4 = 80$ ft^2; total painting surface: 780 ft^2 **2. a.** $82{,}247 \cdot 0.004 = \$328.99$ **b.** paint: $780 \div 250 = 3.12$ gal; $2 \cdot 3.12 \cdot 36 = \$224.64$ roof: $2\left(\dfrac{\sqrt{116}}{3} \cdot 5\right) \approx 35.90$ yd^2 $35.90 \cdot 42 = \$1507.80$ shed: \$1732.44	**20** Total possible points **5** for each part with shown work and the correct answer with appropriate label; Deduct points for minor errors or missing work or labels.
3. cost of shed and water: \$2061.43 $2061.43 + 28{,}934 = \$30{,}995.43$; Students need to provide some means to compensate for the start-up costs. *Sample answer:* On a day with an average attendance of 180 people at an admission cost of \$16 with an open number of days of 90 would sum to \$259,200. An estimated cost of 20 workers for a day of 7 hours at an average cost of \$10 per hour is \$1400. Also, 90 days times the estimated operating costs of employees, plus water, shed, and additional renovation costs is approximately $126{,}000 + 30{,}995.43 = \$156{,}995.43$. So, at least 20 people have jobs, kids have a place to go, and there could be a profit after estimated expenses.	**10** Correct answer for total cost and some plan for the income if the park reopens, including an estimate of operating costs **5** About half of the factors are accounted for and the plan is not complete, but there are some correct factors.
Mathematics Practice: Students make a reasonable argument to support the renovation and reopening of the waterpark.	**3** Students have a plan to make sure that the costs cover the renovations (it does not have to be completely covered in the first year). Partial credit can be awarded.
Total Points	**33 points**

Name_____ Date_____

Chapter 11 Performance Task (continued)

Waterpark Renovation

The city council will consider reopening the closed water park if your team can come up with a cost analysis for painting some of the structures, filling the pool water reservoirs, and resurfacing some of the surfaces. What is your plan to convince the city council to open the water park?

1. Your class decides that each member should work on different parts of the plan. Use the information provided to calculate your part of the proposal. Remember to document the information so your classmates can check your work.

   a. The lazy river is basically a large circle that will need to be filled with water. The radius of the outer perimeter is 30 yards. The river is 4 feet deep and its width is 5 feet. First compute the river's volume in cubic feet and then calculate how many gallons of water it will hold. Remember 1 cubic foot ≈ 7.48 gallons.

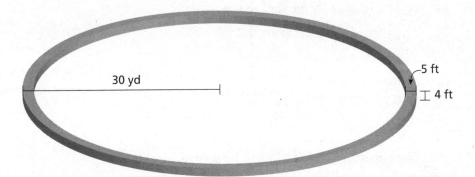

   b. The large decorative storage unit needs to be updated, painted, and re-shingled. The base of the storage shed is a rectangle measuring 15 feet by 20 feet, and the shed's height is 10 feet. The roof's front face is an isosceles triangle with a height of 4 feet. Find the surface area to be painted (including the front and back of the roof's front face).

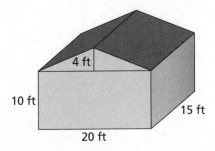

Geometry **159**
Assessment Book

Name _____ Date _____

Waterpark Renovation

2. Using the information you just found, calculate the cost of your section.

   a. The water costs $0.004 per gallon. How much will it cost to fill the entire lazy river?

   b. If you need 2 coats of paint, if the paint costs $36 per gallon, and if a gallon covers approximately 250 square feet, what would be the cost of the paint? The roofing costs $42 per roofing square (square yard). Show your work and explain the cost you came up with for the storage shed update.

3. The rest of your class came up with a cost of $28,934 for their share of the expenses. Add in your costs and explain to the city council why they need to reopen the waterpark and how they can make their money back.

Performance Task (continued)

Teacher Notes:

Name_____ Date_____

1. You randomly draw a marble out of a bag containing 4 green marbles, 6 blue marbles, 8 yellow marbles, and 2 red marbles. Find the probability of drawing a marble that is not yellow.

Find $P(\overline{A})$.

2. $P(A) = 0.53$ 3. $P(A) = \frac{4}{7}$ 4. $P(A) = 0.02$

5. You roll a six-sided die 25 times. A 4 is rolled 6 times. What is the theoretical probability of rolling a 4? What is the experimental probability of rolling a 4?

6. Events A and B are independent. Find the missing probability.

   $P(A) = 0.30$

   $P(B) = $ ____

   $P(A \text{ and } B) = 0.08$

7. Events A and B are dependent. Find the missing probability.

   $P(A) = 0.5$

   $P(B \mid A) = 0.35$

   $P(A \text{ and } B) = $ ____

8. Find the probability that a dart thrown at the circular target shown will hit the given region. Assume the dart is equally likely to hit any point inside the target.

   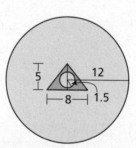

   a. the center circle

   b. outside the triangle

   c. inside the triangle but outside the center circle

9. There are 8 men and 12 women working for a company. The company allows its workers to vote between two benefit packages. A total of 5 men and 4 women vote for the first benefit package. Find and interpret the marginal frequencies.

Answers

1. _____

2. _____

3. _____

4. _____

5. _____

     _____

6. _____

7. _____

8. a._____

    b._____

    c._____

9. _____

     _____

     _____

     _____

     _____

     _____

Chapter 12 Test A

You roll a die. Find the probability of the event described.

Answers

1. You roll a 5.

2. You roll a prime number.

3. You roll a multiple of 2.

4. You roll a number greater than 6.

Evaluate the expression.

5. $_5C_2$ **6.** $_7P_3$ **7.** $_8C_4$ **8.** $_8P_4$

9. You are looking to choose a cable company to provide service at your house. Four companies all offer identical packages at the same price. You have surveyed many people in your neighborhood to find out if they are satisfied with their current cable package that each company produces. The table below shows the results of the survey you conducted. Based on these results, what cable company should you choose?

	Company 1	Company 2	Company 3	Company 4
Satisfied	卌 |||	||||	卌		卌
Not Satisfied	|||	||	||||	||

1. _____
2. _____
3. _____
4. _____
5. _____
6. _____
7. _____
8. _____
9. _____
10. __See left.__
11. a._____

      b._____

      c._____

10. For events A and B, $P(A) = \frac{3}{14}$ and $P(B) = \frac{1}{5}$. Also, $P(A \text{ and } B) = \frac{3}{65}$. Are A and B independent events? Explain your answer below.

11. A game at the state fair has a circular target with a radius of 12 centimeters on a square board measuring 30 centimeters a side, as shown. Players win if they are able to throw a dart and hit the circular area only.

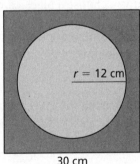

r = 12 cm

30 cm

  a. What is the probability that a dart will hit the circular region?

  b. What is the probability that a dart will hit the square region that is outside the circle?

  c. In order for a player to win a prize, that player must hit the circular region with 3 consecutive darts (darts removed after each toss). What is the probability of a player winning a prize?

Chapter 12 **Test A** (continued)

12. According to a survey done at your school, about 42% of all the female students participate in 2 sport seasons. You randomly ask 5 female students at your school how many sport seasons they participate in.

   a. Draw a histogram of the Binomial distribution for this survey below.

   b. What is the most likely outcome to this survey?

   c. What is the probability that at least 3 of the 5 female students surveyed participate in 2 sport seasons?

13. Consider a shuffled set of 52 playing cards. The kind of cards that are in the set is listed in the table below.

	Ace	King	Queen	Jack	Non-face card
Black	2	2	2	2	18
Red	2	2	2	2	18

   a. You choose one card at random from the shuffled deck. Find the probability that you choose a black card or a jack.

   b. You choose one card at random, do not replace it, and then choose a second card at random. Find the probability that you choose a non-face card followed by a queen.

14. There are 15 students (including you) in your Student Council activity. Your closest friends in the activity are Rachel and Randall. Three students must be picked by your teacher of the activity.

   a. What is the probability that you, Rachel, and Randall are picked by the teacher?

   b. The first student chosen will become the President, the second student chosen will become the Vice President, and the third student chosen will become the Treasurer. What is the probability that you will be picked as the President, Rachel will be picked as the Vice President, and Randall will be picked as the Treasurer?

Answers

12. a.___See left.___

b._____

c._____

13. a._____

b._____

14. a._____

b._____

Chapter 12 Test B

You spin a spinner that has equal spots numbered 1–8. Find the probability of the event described.

Answers

1. You spin a 4.

2. You spin a composite number.

3. You spin a multiple of 2.

4. You spin a number less than 1.

Evaluate the expression.

5. $_{12}P_5$ 6. $_7C_4$ 7. $_{13}C_7$ 8. $_9P_4$

9. You are researching a method to determine what will give you the best chance of passing your driver's test. All 3 options for passing the test will cost you the same amount of money. You ask all your friends who have been involved in one of these 3 options. The table shows the results of your research. Based on this information, what method will give you the best chance to pass the driver's test?

	Passed	Not Passed
Book Class	18	6
Driver's School	31	11
Internet Class	8	3

10. Is it possible to use the formula $P(A \text{ and } B) = P(B) \bullet P(A \mid B)$? Explain your reasoning below.

1. _____

2. _____

3. _____

4. _____

5. _____

6. _____

7. _____

8. _____

9. _____

10. ___See left.___

11. a._____

    b._____

    c._____

11. You are playing a game similar to shuffleboard, where you need to slide a puck into the light gray area of the board in order to score points. The board is surrounded by wood boards that keep the puck in the playing surface. An image of the board and its dimensions are shown to the right.

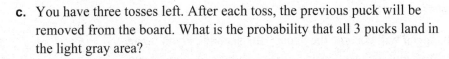

4 feet   1.5 feet

12 feet

5 feet

a. What is the probability that you slide the puck into the light gray area?

b. What is the probability that you slide the puck into the dark gray area?

c. You have three tosses left. After each toss, the previous puck will be removed from the board. What is the probability that all 3 pucks land in the light gray area?

Chapter 12 **Test B** (continued)

12. According to a survey, about 53% of all teenagers under the age of 13 now own a cell phone. You ask 7 randomly chosen teenagers under the age of 13 whether they currently own a cell phone.

a. Draw a histogram of the Binomial distribution for this survey below.

b. What is the most likely outcome to this survey?

c. What is the probability that at least 4 out of 7 teenagers under the age of 13 own a cell phone?

13. A small bag contains 6 pennies, 5 nickels, 3 dimes, 5 quarters, and 2 one-dollar coins.

a. You choose one coin at random from the bag. What is the probability that you choose a one-dollar coin or a dime?

b. You choose one coin at random, replace it, and then choose a second coin at random. What is the probability that you first choose a nickel and then choose a penny?

c. You choose one coin at random, do not replace it, and then choose a second coin at random. What is the probability that you choose a quarter followed by another quarter?

14. While at a family reunion, you are blindfolded to play a game called "tag." In this game, the person who is blindfolded must tag 3 people before their turn has ended. There are 21 people playing the game, including you, your sister, your brother, and your friend.

a. What is the probability that while you are blindfolded, you tag your sister, brother, and friend?

b. The first person tagged will become the "goat," the second person tagged will be the "donkey," and the last person tagged will become the "sheep" in the game. What is the probability that you tag your sister as the "goat," your brother as the "donkey," and your friend as the "sheep?"

Answers

12. a. _____See left._____

b._____

c._____

13. a._____

b._____

c._____

14. a._____

b._____

Chapter 12 Alternative Assessment

1. For a carnival game, a turn consists of spinning the spinner shown twice. If the product of the two numbers is odd, you win. If the product of the two numbers is even, you lose. In addition, if the product of the two numbers is prime, you win a grand prize. The assistant assures you that the odds are in your favor because you are more likely to land on an odd number.

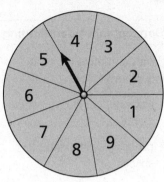

a. Are you more likely to land on an odd or even number? Explain. Does this imply you are more likely to win on your turn? Explain.

b. Are the two spins independent or dependent events? Explain.

c. How many possible outcomes (consisting of two spins) are there?

d. List the sample space of possible outcomes.

e. What is the probability of the product of the two numbers being odd?

f. What is the probability of the product of the two numbers being even?

g. Is this a fair game? Explain.

h. Describe one possible grand prize turn. What can you say about the values of the two spins?

i. Suppose you have a grand prize turn with the first spin landing on 1 and the second spin landing on a prime. Using area, what is the probability of this grand prize turn? Now, suppose you have a grand prize turn with the first spin landing on a prime and the second spin landing on a 1, what is the probability of this grand prize turn? Using what you know about disjoint events, what is the probability of winning the grand prize? Verify this using your sample space.

j. How could you change the rules of this game to make it more fair?

k. Using the original rules, how could you change the board of this game to make it more fair?

Chapter 12 Alternative Assessment Rubric

Score	Conceptual Understanding	Mathematical Skills	Work Habits
4	Shows complete understanding of: • independent and dependent events • probability and sample space	All answers are correct and explanations are correct and thorough.	Answers all parts of all problems Answers are explained thoroughly with mathematical terminology. Work is very neat and well organized.
3	Shows nearly complete understanding of: • independent and dependent events • probability and sample space	One answer is incorrect but all explanations show correct reasoning and are thorough.	Answers most parts of all problems Answers are explained with mathematical terminology. Work is neat and organized.
2	Shows some understanding of: • independent and dependent events • probability and sample space	Two to three answers are incorrect. Explanations may show incorrect reasoning but are still complete.	Answers some parts of all problems Answers are poorly or incorrectly explained. Work is not very neat or organized.
1	Shows little understanding of: • independent and dependent events • probability and sample space	Four or more answers are incorrect, and explanations are completely incorrect or missing.	Attempts few parts of any problem No explanation is included with answers. Work is sloppy and disorganized.

Name_____ Date _____

Chapter 12 Performance Task

A New Dartboard

Instructional Overview	
Launch Question	You are a graphic artist working for a company on a new design for the board in the game of darts. You are eager to begin the project, but the team cannot decide on the terms of the game. Everyone agrees that the board should have four colors. But some want the probabilities of hitting each color to be equal, while others want them to be different. You offer to design two boards, one for each group. How do you get started? How creative can you be with your designs?
Summary	Students use geometric probabilities to design two dart boards with different specifications.
Teacher Notes	Students may not be familiar with the design of an old-fashioned dart board, so it may be helpful to have one in the classroom or a picture to share with the students. It also may be helpful to have pictures of different game boards for student reference.
	Students sometimes have preconceived ideas that confuse symmetry with equal probability, and that is one emphasis of this task—that while the two concepts can sometimes occur together, they are not the same and often do not occur together. Encourage students to think of a way to color a symmetrical design that would show a different area ratio for each color. Encourage them to think of a non-symmetrical design that could be colored so that the colors do have an equal amount of area in the design.
Supplies	Handouts, drawing and coloring supplies, different types of paper, cardboard, or poster board (optional)
Mathematical Discourse	What are some common board games? Which ones have the most visually appealing game boards? Why?
Writing/Discussion Prompts	If you were to purchase one of your game boards, which would it be? Why?

Curriculum Content	
Content Objectives	• Find sample spaces (the sets of all possible outcomes) of probability experiments. • Find theoretical probabilities that events will occur.
Mathematical Practices	• Construct a viable argument for the designs of the dartboards and listen to the reasoning of others.

Chapter 12 **Performance Task** (continued)

Rubric

A New Dartboard	Points
Board is based on 4 colors.	**3 points**
For one board, each of the four colors covers the same area of the board, so they have an equal probability of being hit. For the other board, each of the four colors covers a different area of the board, so they do not have an equal probability of being hit.	**10** Both boards satisfy the requirements. **5** One board satisfies the requirements. **1** Neither board satisfies the requirements.
Worksheet questions are answered correctly. 1. *Sample answer:* red, yellow, green, and blue 2. *Sample answer:* The total area of each color must be the same for the equal probability board, and the area for at least 1 color must be unequal for the other board. 3. *Sample answer:* The shape of either board can be symmetric or non-symmetric. The important thing about the shape is that you must be able to calculate the area of each color on the board. 4. *Sample answer:* The sections do not have to have the same shape, but you must be able to calculate the area of each one. 5–6. Answers will vary with each board.	
The explanations for the probabilities on each board are well-written and thoroughly explained using area. The explanations are supported with calculations using geometric probabilities.	**10** The explanations and calculations are correct. **5** Explanations are correct but the calculations are incorrect. **1** Neither the explanations nor the calculations are correct.
Mathematics Practice: Construct viable arguments and critique the reasoning of others.	**2** For demonstration of practice partial credit can be awarded.
Total Points	**25 points**

Performance Task (continued)

A New Dartboard

You are a graphic artist working for a company on a new design for the board in the game of darts. You are eager to begin the project, but the team cannot decide on the terms of the game. Everyone agrees that the board should have four colors. But some want the probabilities of hitting each color to be equal, while others want them to be different. You offer to design two boards, one for each group. How do you get started? How creative can you be with your designs?

1. What 4 colors will you use for your board? Will it have a theme or a specific name?

2. How will you make sure that all four colors on one board have the same theoretical probability of being hit and that the colors on the other board do not have the same probability of being hit?

3. How will you choose the shape of your boards? What is important about the shape? Does the board with equal color probabilities have to be symmetrical? Does the board with unequal color probabilities have to be non-symmetrical? Explain.

4. How many sections will you have on each board? What is the minimum number of sections? How will you shape the sections of your boards? Do the sections on the board with equal probability need to be the same shape? Why or why not?

5. How will players score points using your board? Will each section be worth the same amount of points?

6. Calculate the probabilities of hitting each color on your board. Use mathematics to show that each color on one board has an equal probability of being hit and that colors on the other board do not have an equal probability of being hit.

Chapters 10–12 **Cumulative Test**

1. Classify each angle as specifically as possible.

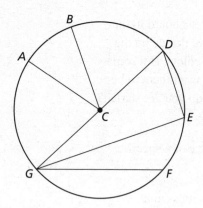

   a. ∠ACB   **b.** ∠DGE   **c.** ∠GED   **d.** ∠EGF

2. Copy and complete the paragraph proof.

   Given   Circle C with center $(4, 3)$ and radius 3,

             Circle D with center $(1, 2)$ and radius 1

   Prove   Circle C is similar to Circle D.

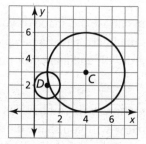

Map Circle C to Circle C' by using the _____ $(x, y) \rightarrow$ _____ so that Circle C' and Circle D have the same center at (____, ____). Dilate Circle C' using a center of dilation (____, ____) and a scale factor of _____. Because there is a set of _____ transformations that map Circle C to Circle D, Circle C is _____ Circle D.

Chapters 10–12 Cumulative Test (continued)

3. Use the diagram to write a proof.

   Given $\angle A$ is supplementary to $\angle CDE$.

   Prove $\triangle ABC \sim \triangle DBE$

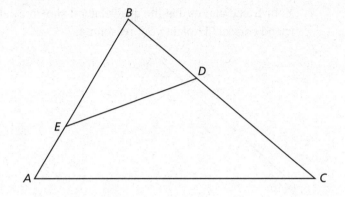

4. The equation of a circle is $x^2 + y^2 - 10x + 12y + 29 = 0$. What are the center and the approximate radius of the circle?

   A. center: $(-5, 6)$, radius: 9.5

   B. center: $(-10, 12)$, radius: 5.4

   C. center: $(5, -6)$, radius: 5.7

   D. center: $(10, -12)$, radius: 5.4

5. The coordinates of the vertices of a quadrilateral are $P(1, 2)$, $Q(7, 2)$, $R(4, -1)$, and $T(-2, -1)$. Prove that quadrilateral $PQRT$ is a parallelogram.

6. Classify each related conditional statement based on the conditional statement, "If you are in Times Square, then you are in New York City."

   a. You are in Times Square if and only if you are in New York City.

   b. If you are not in New York City, then you are not in Times Square.

   c. If you are in New York City, then you are in Times Square.

   d. If you are not in Times Square, then you are not in New York City.

Chapters 10–12 **Cumulative Test** (continued)

7. Your friend claims that the quadrilateral shown can be inscribed in a circle. Is your friend correct? Explain your reasoning.

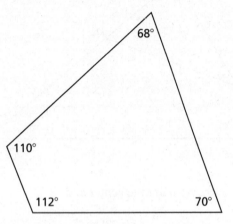

8. Use the diagram. $\overrightarrow{DE}$ and $\overrightarrow{AE}$ are tangent to C.

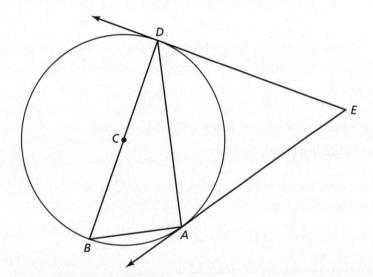

  a. Find $m\angle DAB$.

  b. If $m\overset{\frown}{BA} = 70°$, find $m\angle DBA$.

  c. If $m\overset{\frown}{ABD} = 260°$, find $m\angle E$.

  d. If $m\angle EDA = 50°$, find $m\overset{\frown}{DA}$.

Chapters 10–12 Cumulative Test (continued)

9. Identify the shape of the cross section formed by the intersection of the plane and the solid.

   a.

   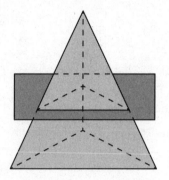

   b.

   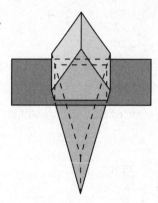

10. In the figure, $QR = ST$, $\overline{UP} \perp \overline{QR}$, and $\overline{VP} \perp \overline{ST}$. What must be true about UP and VP? Select all that apply.

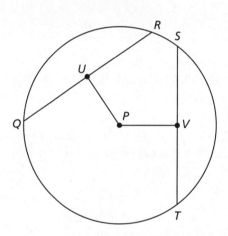

$UP = VP$	$UP = \frac{1}{2}QR$	$\overline{UP} \perp \overline{VP}$	$VP = \frac{1}{2}ST$

Name _____ Date _____

11. What is the equation of the line passing through the point $(6, 2)$ that is perpendicular to the line $2x + \frac{1}{3}y = -5$?

 A. $y = -6x + 38$ B. $y = 6x - 34$

 C. $y = -\frac{1}{6}x + 3$ D. $y = \frac{1}{6}x + 1$

12. A silo is a composite of a cylinder and half a sphere. What is the approximate volume of the silo?

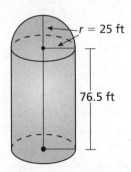

 $r = 25$ ft

 76.5 ft

 A. $215{,}657.25$ ft^3 B. $182{,}932.32$ ft^3

 C. $232{,}019.71$ ft^3 D. $150{,}207.40$ ft^3

13. Prove or disprove that the point $\left(4, \sqrt{2}\right)$ lies on the circle centered at the origin and containing the point $(3, 3)$.

14. The diagram shows a right circular cylinder and a rectangular prism with a square base. Both have the same height, h, and the base of the rectangular prism has side length s. According to Cavalieri's Principle, the solids will have the same volume if the circular base of the cylinder has radius _____.

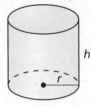
h
r

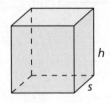
h
s

Chapters 10–12 **Cumulative Test** (continued)

15. Your friend claims that if you rotate the figure around the given axis, the composite solid will be made of a right circular cylinder and a cone. Is your friend correct? Explain your reasoning.

16. According to a survey, 37% of American households hire a lawn care service. You randomly select 12 American households to survey.

   a. Draw a histogram of the binomial distribution of the number of households out of the 12 you selected that hire a lawn care service.

   b. What is the most likely number of households out of the 12 you selected that hire a lawn care service?

   c. What is the approximate probability that at most 6 households out of the 12 you selected hire a lawn care service? Round your answer to the nearest hundredth.

17. A survey asked male and female students about whether they prefer Sign Language class or French class. The table shows the results of the survey.

		Class		
		Sign Language	French	Total
Gender	Female		19	
	Male			43
	Total	54		95

   a. Complete the two-way table.

   b. What is the probability that a randomly selected student is male and prefers French class?

   c. What is the probability that a randomly selected female student prefers sign language?

Name _____ Date _____

Find the length of $\overline{ST}$.

Answers

1.

S•——27——•M————58————•T

2.

|———47———|
S•——————•T 19 M 15 •O

3. $J(-3, 7)$ and $K(4, -2)$ are endpoints of a line segment. Find the coordinates of the midpoint M. Find the distance between the endpoints of $\overline{JK}$.

4. The midpoint of JK is $M(2, 5)$. One endpoint is $J(-4, 2)$. Find the coordinates of endpoint K. Find the distance between the endpoints of $\overline{JK}$.

Use the diagram to decide whether the statement is true or false.

5. Points G, C, and H are collinear.

6. Plane S and plane T intersect at line m.

7. Points A, B, and C lie on plane T.

8. $\overline{CG}$ and $\overline{FE}$ are opposite rays.

9. Point C lies on plane S and plane T.

10. Plane S is perpendicular to plane T.

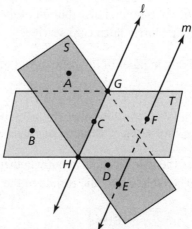

Solve the equation.

11. $9x - 16 = 7x + 12$

12. $5(3x + 2) = -6x - 11$

Find the value of x or y. State which theorems or postulates you used.

13.

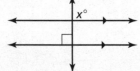

14.

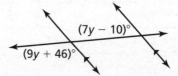

Find the value of x that makes $m \parallel n$.

15.

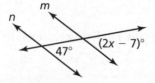

16.

m
n

$(2x - 7)°$

$47°$

Write an equation of the line that passes through the given point and is (a) parallel to and (b) perpendicular to the given line.

17. $(-2, -1)$, $y = -3x + 2$

18. $(-3, 1)$, $x = 0$

Answers

1. _____

2. _____

3. _____

   _____

4. _____

   _____

5. _____

6. _____

7. _____

8. _____

9. _____

10. _____

11. _____

12. _____

13. _____

    _____

14. _____

    _____

    _____

15. _____

16. _____

17. a._____

    b._____

18. a._____

    b._____

Post Course **Post Course Test** (continued)

Graph triangle △*MEG* with vertices *M*(1, 1), *E*(5, 3), and *G*(3, 5) and its image

after the translation.

Answers

19. $(x, y) \rightarrow (x - 1, y - 2)$

20. $(x, y) \rightarrow (x + 3, y - 6)$

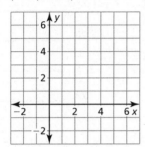

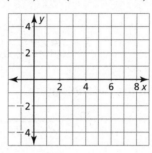

19. __See left.__

20. __See left.__

21. __See left.__

22. __See left.__

23. _____

_____

_____

_____

Graph the polygon with the given vertices and its image after a rotation of the

given number of degrees about the origin.

21. $M(-4, 4), L(-5, 1), K(-2, 2);$ 180°

22. $M(0, 0), E(-2, -2), T(-1, 4),$ $S(2, -3); 270°$

24. _____

_____

_____

_____

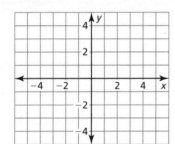

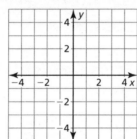

25. _____

26. _____

Find the measure of each angle.

23.

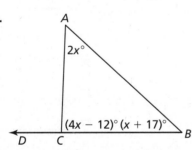

24.

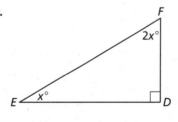

$\overline{TU}$ is a midsegment of △*QRS*. Find the value of *x*.

25.

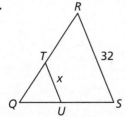

26.

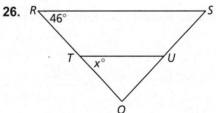

Name _____ Date _____

Post Course **Post Course Test** (continued)

Find AC. Identify the theorem you used.

27.

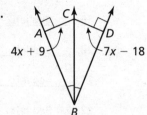

28.

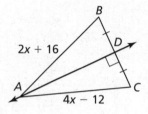

Find the value of each variable in the parallelogram.

29.

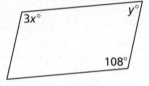

30.

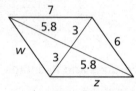

Give the most specific name for the quadrilateral. Explain your reasoning.

31.

32.

Determine whether the triangles are similar. If they are, write a similarity statement.

33.

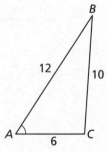

Find the value of the variable

34.

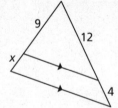

35.

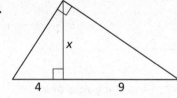

Find the value of each variable. Round your answers to the nearest tenth.

36.

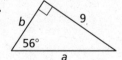

37.

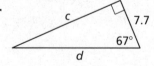

Answers

27. _____

_____

28. _____

_____

29. _____

_____

30. _____

_____

31. _____

_____

_____

32. _____

_____

_____

33. _____

_____

34. _____

35. _____

36. _____

37. _____

180 **Geometry**
Assessment Book

Copyright © Big Ideas Learning, LLC
All rights reserved.

Name_____ Date _____

Post Course Test (continued)

Solve △ABC. Round decimal answers to the nearest tenth.

Answers

38.

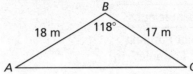

39.

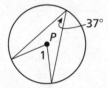

38. _____

39. _____

40. _____

Find the value of the variable or the measure of the numbered angle in ⊙P.

41. _____

40.

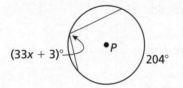

41.

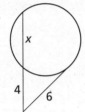

42. _____

43. _____

Find the value of the variable.

44. _____

42.

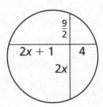

43.

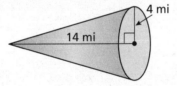

45. _____

46. _____

47. _____

Find the volume of the solid.

44.

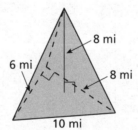

45.

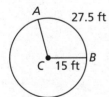

Find the indicated measure.

46. $m\overarc{AB}$

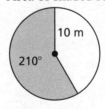

47. Area of shaded sector

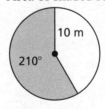

Post Course Test Item Analysis

Item Number	Skills
1	finding segment lengths
2	finding segment lengths
3	using Midpoint Formula and Distance Formula
4	using Midpoint Formula and Distance Formula
5	properties of lines and points in planes
6	properties of lines and points in planes
7	properties of lines and points in planes
8	properties of lines and points in planes
9	properties of lines and points in planes
10	properties of lines and points in planes
11	solving equations
12	solving equations
13	working with parallel lines
14	working with parallel lines
15	working with parallel lines
16	working with parallel lines
17	writing equations of lines
18	writing equations of lines
19	transforming polygons
20	transforming polygons
21	transforming polygons
22	transforming polygons
23	properties of triangles
24	properties of triangles
25	properties of triangles

Item Number	Skills
26	properties of triangles
27	properties of triangles
28	properties of triangles
29	properties of parallelograms
30	properties of parallelograms
31	properties of parallelograms
32	properties of parallelograms
33	similar triangles
34	similar triangles
35	similar triangles
36	solving right triangles
37	solving right triangles
38	solving triangles
39	solving triangles
40	properties of circles
41	properties of circles
42	properties of circles
43	properties of circles
44	finding volume of a solid
45	finding volume of a solid
46	finding arc length
47	finding sector area

Answers

Prerequisite Skills Test

1. 4 **2.** 7 **3.** 7 **4.** 17

5. 1 **6.** 14 **7.** 11 **8.** 11

9. 11 **10.** 42 m^2 **11.** 67.5 ft^2 **12.** 56 cm^2

13. $a_n = 2n$; 80 **14.** $a_n = 4n - 9$; 151

15. $a_n = 1.5n + 2.6$; 62.6 **16.** $a_n = -9n + 90$; -270

17. $a_n = -7n + 13$; -267 **18.** $a_n = \frac{1}{4}n$; 10

19. $x = y - \frac{1}{3}$ **20.** $x = \frac{3}{4}y - 3$

21. $x = \frac{2}{5}y - \frac{14}{5}$ **22.** $x = -\frac{1}{2}y + 3$

23. $x = \dfrac{y - 5}{z - 2}$ **24.** $x = \dfrac{z}{3 + 2y}$

25. -2 **26.** $\frac{4}{3}$ **27.** undefined

28. $y = -x + 5$ **29.** $x = -1$

30. $y = 3x - 3$ **31.** $y = 3$

32. $y = -\frac{5}{2}x - 4$ **33.** $y = \frac{1}{2}x - 2$

34. dilation **35.** reflection

36. rotation **37.** translation

38. yes; Corresponding sides are proportional.

39. no; Corresponding sides are not proportional.

40. $x = -1$ **41.** $y = 1$ **42.** $m = 16$

43. $w = 2$ **44.** $x = -3$ **45.** $g = 0$

46. $M = \left(-\frac{1}{2}, 3\right)$; $D = \sqrt{113} \approx 10.63$

47. $M = \left(-\frac{3}{2}, -\frac{1}{2}\right)$; $D = \sqrt{130} \approx 11.40$

48. $y = -2x + 8$ **49.** $x = 6$

50. $y = \frac{3}{2}x + \frac{17}{2}$ **51.** $6 < x < 10$

52. $y \leq 2$ or $y \geq 5$ **53.** $b \leq -4$ or $b > 0$

54. $-7 < k < -1$ **55.** $x = 1$

56. $x = 4$ **57.** $x = 5$

58. $x = 1$ **59.** line 1 || line 2

60. line 1 || line 2, line 3 || line 4, lines 1 and 2 are perpendicular to lines 3 and 4

61. $4\sqrt{3}$ **62.** $6\sqrt{6}$ **63.** $6\sqrt{3}$ **64.** $\frac{5\sqrt{3}}{3}$

65. $4\sqrt{2}$ **66.** $2\sqrt{5}$ **67.** yes **68.** no

69. yes **70.** $k = 18$

71. $k = 28$ **72.** $a = -\frac{1}{6}$

73. $x^2 + 6x + 8$ **74.** $m^2 - 7m + 10$

75. $5x^2 - 3x - 2$ **76.** $4g^2 + 19g - 5$

77. $x^2 - 81$ **78.** $5 + 13a - 6a^2$

79. $m = -4$, $m = -16$ **80.** $y = 5.11$, $y = -13.11$

81. $x = 7.06$, $x = -11.06$

82. $m = 7$, $m = -5$

83. 228 cm^2 **84.** 216 in.^{2}

85. 216 ft^2 **86.** 14 m

87. 14.5 cm **88.** $6\sqrt{2} \approx 8.5$ ft

Pre-Course Test

1. 25 **2.** 46

3. $M(-1, 9)$; $D = 4\sqrt{2} \approx 5.7$ units

4. $G(-2, 23)$; $D = 2\sqrt{305} \approx 34.9$ units

5. false **6.** true **7.** true **8.** false

9. true **10.** false **11.** $x = -3$ **12.** $x = 1$

13. 56; Corresponding Angles Theorem (Thm. 3.1)

14. 20; Consecutive Interior Angles Theorem (Thm. 3.4)

15. 101 **16.** 24

17. a. $y = 2x - 3$ **b.** $y = -\frac{1}{2}x - \frac{11}{2}$

Answers

18. a. $y = \frac{1}{5}x - 3$ **b.** $y = -5x + 23$

19. 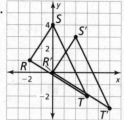   **20.**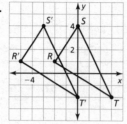

21.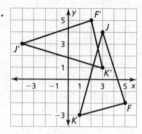

22.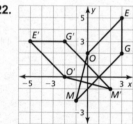

23. $m\angle X = 67°$, $m\angle Y = 23°$

24. $m\angle A = 60°$, $m\angle B = 60°$, $m\angle C = 60°$

25. 18   **26.** 8

27. 14; Perpendicular Bisector Theorem (Thm. 6.1)

28. 24; Angle Bisector Theorem (Thm. 6.3)

29. $x = 115$, $y = 65$ **30.** $a = 8$, $b = 10$

31. rhombus; all 4 sides are equal but no right angles

32. isosceles trapezoid; base angles congruent, top and bottom bases parallel

33. no; Only one diagonal is bisected, but both need to be bisected.

34. yes; Parallelogram Consecutive Angles Theorem (Thm. 7.5)

35. yes; $\triangle LMN \cong \triangle QRS$

36. 6   **37.** about 6.7

38. $a = 4.2$, $b = 6.8$

39. $a = $ about 3, $b = $ about 6.2

40. $m\angle 1 = 80°$, $m\angle 2 = 40°$

41. $m\angle 1 = 110°$, $m\angle 2 = 70°$

42. 16   **43.** 9

44. about 1407.4 km^3 **45.** 270 km^3

46. about 120°   **47.** about 117.8 in.^{2}

Chapter 1

1.1–1.3 Quiz

1. *Sample answer:* plane R and plane AED

2. points A, B, and C

3. *Sample answer:* points A, B, and D

4. *Sample answer:* points A, E, and D

5. *Sample answer:* $\overrightarrow{BA}$

6. *Sample answer:* line ℓ and line $\overleftrightarrow{AC}$

7. *Sample answer:* $\overline{BD}$

8.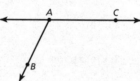

9.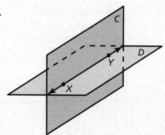

10. 28   **11.** 56   **12.** $(-3, 4.5)$

13. $2\sqrt{10}$ **14.** line ℓ; 32   **15.** $(10, -8)$

A2   **Geometry**
Answers

Answers

Test A

1. 18 units; $XY = XZ + ZY$, because point Z is on $\overline{XY}$.

2. 154 mi

3. $x = 17.5$; $LN = 105$

4. *Sample answer:* $\overrightarrow{XR}$

5. *Sample answer:* points T, Q, and P

6. *Sample answer:* points T, R, and Y

7. *Sample answer:* plane TRP

8.

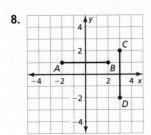

$\overline{AB} \approx \overline{CD}$

9. $\left(4, -\frac{1}{2}\right)$

10. $(8, -2)$

11. perimeter $= 32$ units, area $= 60$ square units

12. line ℓ; $XY = 14$ units

13. $\overline{ML}$; $XY = 18$ units

14. $m\angle DBC = 57°$, $m\angle ABC = 114°$

15. $m\angle DBC = 70°$, $m\angle ABC = 140°$

16. $m\angle ABD = 55°$, $m\angle DBC = 55°$

17. $114.8°$

18. $24.8°$

19. $(182 - 3x)°$

20. $(92 - 3x)°$

Test B

1. *Sample answer:* plane QSU

2. *Sample answer:* $\overrightarrow{MP}$

3. *Sample answer:* $\overrightarrow{QT}$, $\overrightarrow{NP}$

4. *Sample answer:* point O

5. 188 mi

6. $\left(-\frac{3}{2}, 7\right)$

7. $\left(\frac{9}{2}, -\frac{3}{2}\right)$

8. $C(7, 5)$

9. $E(2, 5)$

10. point S; $RT = 20$

11. a.

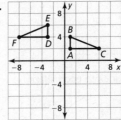

b. Each triangle has an area of 5 square units.

c. yes; They are congruent triangles.

12. $30°$; acute

13. $70°$; acute

14. $100°$; obtuse

15. $99.5°$

16. $82.75°$

17. *Sample answer:* $\angle LPN$, $\angle LPM$, $\angle MPN$; alternate names include $\angle P$, $\angle NPL$, $\angle NPM$, $\angle MPL$

18. One angle is $52°$ and the other is $38°$.

Alternative Assessment

1. a. $\overrightarrow{CF}$

   b. point F

   c. *Sample answer:* plane ABF, plane CDE, plane BCD

   d. $\overrightarrow{AB}$

   e. straight angle

   f. method 1: Find the total area of two 9-inch by 12-inch rectangles. Because the segments are congruent, $AF = FE$ and $AB = ED$; method 2: Find the total area of one 18-inch by 12-inch rectangle. $AE = 18$ by the Segment Addition Postulate (Post. 1.2). *Sample answer:* method 2 because it involves less steps

2. a. octagon; concave; *Sample answer:* $\overleftrightarrow{AC}$ contains points in the exterior of the polygon.

   b. $(6.5, 7)$

   c. $\overline{CD} \cong \overline{FE}$, $\overline{CB} \cong \overline{FG}$, $\overline{AB} \cong \overline{HG}$

   d. about $101.3°$

   e.

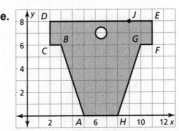

   f. the first design; The perimeter of the first design (about 30.2 units) is less than the perimeter of the second design (about 30.6 units).

Answers

Chapter 2

2.1–2.3 Quiz

1. consecutive perfect squares; 36, 49

2. adding two additional sides to each shape;

3. If the clock strikes 12, then it is noon; converse: If it is noon, then the clock strikes 12; inverse: If the clock does not strike 12, then it is not noon; contrapositive: If it is not noon, then the clock does not strike 12; The if-then statement and the contrapositive are false, and the converse and inverse are true.

4. If an angle measures 87°, then it is an acute angle; converse: If an angle is acute, then it measures 87°; inverse: If an angle does not measure 87°, then it is not an acute angle; contrapositive: If an angle is not acute, then it does not measure 87°; The if-then statement and the contrapositive are true, and the converse and inverse are false.

5. If this month is December, then next month is November; converse: If the next month is November, then this month is December; inverse: If this month is not December, then next month is not November; contrapositive: If the next month is not November; then this month is not December; all are false

6. *Sample answer:* $-11 - 5 = -16$

7. *Sample answer:* a 30°-60°-90° triangle

8. The quotient of two negative numbers is positive; *Sample answer:* $\dfrac{-n}{-m} = \dfrac{n}{m}$

9. The sum of the absolute values of any two numbers is nonnegative; *Sample answer:* For any numbers m and n, $|m| \geq 0$ and $|n| \geq 0$, so $|m| + |n| \geq 0$.

10. no   11. yes   12. no

13. yes   14. yes

Test A

1. false   2. true   3. false

4. true   5. true   6. true

7. false; If two planes intersect, then their intersection is a line. Plane Intersection Postulate (Post. 2.7).

8. true

9. converse: If it is the weekend, then it is Sunday; inverse: If it is not Sunday, then it is not the weekend.

10. converse: If $\angle A$ is obtuse, then $m\angle A = 95°$; inverse: If $m\angle A \neq 95°$, then $\angle A$ is not obtuse.

11. converse: If an animal has two eyes, then it is a bird; inverse: If an animal is not a bird, then it does not have two eyes.

12. inductive reasoning

13. deductive reasoning

14. Points A, B, and C are collinear.

15. You are not going outdoors.

16. If a quadrilateral is a square, then it is a rectangle.

17. If a number ends in 0, then it is divisible by 5.

18. $x = -19$;

$\dfrac{x + 3}{-2} = 8$	Given
$x + 3 = -16$	Multiplication Property of Equality
$x = -19$	Subtraction Property of Equality

19. $x = -5$;

$5x - 3 = 4(x - 2)$	Given
$5x - 3 = 4x - 8$	Distributive Property
$x - 3 = -8$	Subtraction Property of Equality
$x = -5$	Addition Property of Equality

Answers

20. $P = \dfrac{I}{rt}$; 25000;

$I = Prt$	Given
$7500 = P(0.05)(6)$	Substitution Property of Equality
$7500 = 0.3P$	Simplify.
$25{,}000 = P$	Division Property of Equality

21. Symmetric Property of Segment Congruence (Thm. 2.1)

22. Reflexive Properties of Equality

23. Transitive Properties of Equality

24.

STATEMENTS	REASONS
1. $\angle 1$ and $\angle 2$ are supplementary.	1. Given
2. $m\angle 1 = 135°$	2. Given
3. $m\angle 1 + m\angle 2 = 180°$	3. Definition of supplementary angles
4. $135° + m\angle 2 = 180°$	4. Substitution Property of Equality
5. $m\angle 2 = 45°$	5. Subtraction Property of Equality

Test B

1. If it is 6 P.M., then it is time for dinner.

2. If the measure of an angle is $90°$, then it is a right angle.

3. If two angles are vertical, then they are not adjacent; converse is true

4. If $3x$ is odd, then x is odd; converse is true

5. If the measure of an angle is not $30°$, then it is not an acute angle.

6. If two angles are not supplementary, then their sum is not $180°$.

7. If an animal does not live in the forest, then it is not a panther.

8. If two angles are not congruent, then they do not have the same measure.

9. true   **10.** true   **11.** false   **12.** true

13. $x = 5$;

$-8x + 7 = 33$	Given
$-8x = -40$	Subtraction Property of Equality
$x = 5$	Division Property of Equality

14. $x = 2$;

$9x - 5 = 3x + 7$	Given
$6x - 5 = 7$	Subraction Property of Equality
$6x = 12$	Addition Property of Equality
$x = 2$	Division Property of Equality

15. $x = 3$;

$2(4x - 3) - 8 = 4 + 2x$	Given
$8x - 6 - 8 = 4 + 2x$	Distributive Property
$8x - 14 = 4 + 2x$	Simplify.
$6x - 14 = 4$	Subraction Property of Equality
$6x = 18$	Addition Property of Equality
$x = 3$	Division Property of Equality

16. 5 ft; $w = \dfrac{P - 2\ell}{2}$;

$P = 2\ell + 2w$	Given
$26 = 2(8) + 2w$	Substitution
$26 = 16 + 2w$	Simplify.
$10 = 2w$	Subtraction Property of Equality
$5 = w$	Division Property of Equality

Answers

17. $x = 14$; $m\angle ABD = 59°$, $m\angle DBC = 81°$,
$m\angle ABC = 140°$;

$(5x + 11) + (3x + 17) = 140$	Given
$8x + 28 = 140$	Combine like terms.
$8x = 112$	Subtraction Property of Equality
$x = 14$	Division Property of Equality

$m\angle ABD = 3(14) + 17$; $m\angle ABD = 59°$;
$m\angle DBC = 5(14) + 11$; $m\angle DBC = 81°$

18. deductive reasoning   **19.** inductive reasoning

20. deductive reasoning

21. Symmetric Property of Angle Congruence (Thm. 2.2)

22. Transitive Property of Segment Congruence (Thm. 2.1)

23. Substitution Property of Equality

24. Reflexive Property of Equality

25.

STATEMENTS	REASONS
1. $m\angle 1 + m\angle 2 = 90°$	1. Given
2. $m\angle 3 + m\angle 4 = 90°$	2. Given
3. $m\angle 1 + m\angle 2 = m\angle 3 + m\angle 4$	3. Transitive Property of Equality
4. $m\angle 2 = m\angle 3$	4. Vertical Angles
5. $m\angle 1 + m\angle 2 = m\angle 2 + m\angle 4$	5. Substitution Property of Equality
6. $m\angle 1 = m\angle 4$	6. Subtraction Property of Equality

Alternative Assessment

1. a.

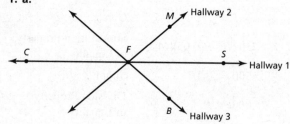

b. at the food court

c. If the clothes are summer clothes, then they are on sale. If the clothes are on sale, then the sale price is 30% off the original price.

d. If the clothes are summer clothes, then the sale price is 30% off the original price.

e. converse: If the sale price is 30% off the original price, then the clothes are summer clothes. inverse: If the clothes are not summer clothes, then the sale price is not 30% off the original price. contrapositive: If the sale price is not 30% off the original price, then the clothes are not summer clothes.

f. acute;
Because $m\angle MFB = m\angle MFS + m\angle SFB$, $m\angle SFB < m\angle MFB$. Because $\angle MFB$ is acute, $m\angle MFB < 90°$, which means that $m\angle SFB < 90°$. So, $\angle SFB$ is acute.

2.

STATEMENTS	REASONS
1. $\angle 3 \cong \angle 2$	1. Given
2. $\angle 1$ and $\angle 2$ are a linear pair.	2. Definition of linear pair
3. $m\angle 1 + m\angle 2 = 180°$	3. Linear Pair Postulate (Post. 2.8)
4. $m\angle 1 + m\angle 3 = 180°$	4. Substitution Property of Equality
5. $\angle 1$ and $\angle 3$ are supplementary.	5. Definition of supplementary angles

Chapter 3

3.1–3.3 Quiz

1. line QR **2.** line RS

3. line KR **4.** plane QRS

5. $\angle 2$ and $\angle 5$, $\angle 4$ and $\angle 7$

Answers

6. ∠2 and ∠7, ∠4 and ∠5

7. ∠1 and ∠5, ∠2 and ∠6, ∠3 and ∠7, ∠4 and ∠8

8. ∠1 and ∠8, ∠3 and ∠6

9. ∠1 and ∠4, ∠2 and ∠3, ∠5 and ∠8, ∠6 and ∠7

10. $m\angle 1 = 65°$, $m\angle 2 = 65°$

11. $m\angle 1 = 131°$, $m\angle 2 = 49°$

12. *Sample answer:* yes; definition of vertical angles, and Consecutive Interior Angles Theorem (Thm. 3.4)

13. *Sample answer:* yes; Corresponding Angles Theorem (Thm. 3.1)

14. $x = 20$ **15.** $x = 29$

Test A

1. *Sample answer:* $\overleftrightarrow{AB}$ and $\overleftrightarrow{CD}$

2. *Sample answer:* $\overleftrightarrow{GE}$ and $\overleftrightarrow{EF}$

3. *Sample answer:* $\overleftrightarrow{AG}$ and $\overleftrightarrow{FE}$

4. *Sample answer:* plane AGH and plane AGE; $\overleftrightarrow{AG}$

5. $x = 32$, $y = 84$; Alternate Exterior Angles Theorem (Thm. 3.3), Linear Pair Postulate (Post. 2.8)

6. $x = 86$, $y = 94$; Alternate Exterior Angles Theorem (Thm. 3.3), Linear Pair Postulate (Post. 2.8)

7. $x = 21$, $y = 29.5$; Corresponding Angles Theorem (Thm. 3.1), Vertical Angles Congruence Theorem (Thm. 2.6)

8. 6   **9.** 7   **10.** 15

11. $p \parallel q$, $\ell \parallel n$; Alternate Interior Angles Converse (Thm. 3.6); both perpendicular to parallel lines

12. $\ell \parallel m$; Consecutive Interior Angles Converse (Thm. 3.8)

13. negative reciprocals   **14.** same

15. perpendicular segment

16. $y = \frac{2}{3}x + 6$ **17.** $y = \frac{2}{7}x - 1$

18. $y = \frac{3}{4}x - 11$ **19.** $y = -4x + 12$

20. $y = \frac{-3}{2}x + 1$ **21.** $y = -\frac{7}{2}x - \frac{35}{2}$

22. $y = \frac{-8}{3}x - 7$ **23.** $y = \frac{1}{4}x + 1$

24. Lines a and b are perpendicular.

25. Lines a and b are parallel. Line c is perpendicular to a and b.

Test B

1. $x = 45$, $y = 49$; Linear Pair Postulate (Post. 2.8), Corresponding Angles Theorem (Thm. 3.1)

2. $x = 23$, $y = 88$; Corresponding Angles Theorem (Thm. 3.1), Linear Pair Postulate (Post. 2.8)

3. $x = 25$, $y = 113$; Alternate Exterior Angles Theorem (Thm. 3.3), Vertical Angles Congruence Theorem (Thm. 2.6)

4. alternate exterior angles, alternate interior angles, corresponding angles

5. consecutive interior angles

6. 45   **7.** 31.5   **8.** 26

9. $y = \frac{1}{2}x - \frac{5}{2}$ **10.** $y = \frac{1}{3}x + 5$

11. $y = \frac{1}{2}x - 4$ **12.** $y = -\frac{3}{2}x + 6$

13. neither   **14.** parallel   **15.** neither

16. perpendicular   **17.** $y = \frac{7}{2}x - \frac{35}{2}$

18 $y = x$ **19.** 7.3 units

20. *Sample answer:* line d and line f

21. *Sample answer:* line d and line a

22. *Sample answer:* $a \parallel b$

23. *Sample answer:* ∠4 and ∠8

Answers

24.

STATEMENTS	REASONS
1. $\ell \parallel m$	1. Given
2. $\angle 1 \cong \angle 3$	2. Corresponding Angles Theorem (Thm. 3.1)
3. $\angle 1 \cong \angle 7$	3. Given
4. $\angle 3 \cong \angle 7$	4. Transitive Property of Angle Congruence (Thm. 2.2)
5. $a \parallel b$	5. Corresponding Angles Converse (Thm. 3.5)

25.

STATEMENTS	REASONS
1. $\angle 5$ and $\angle 2$ are supplementary.	1. Given
2. $m\angle 5 + m\angle 2 = 180°$	2. Definition of supplementary angles
3. $a \parallel b$	3. Given
4. $\angle 1 \cong \angle 5$	4. Corresponding Angles Theorem (Thm. 3.1)
5. $m\angle 1 = m\angle 5$	5. Definition of congruent angles
6. $m\angle 1 + m\angle 2 = 180°$	6. Substitution
7. $\angle 1$ and $\angle 2$ are supplementary.	7. Definition of supplementary angles
8. $\ell \parallel m$	8. Consecutive Interior Angles Converse (Thm. 3.6)

Alternative Assessment

1. a. corresponding angles: $\angle 1$ and $\angle 5$, $\angle 2$ and $\angle 6$, $\angle 3$ and $\angle 7$; $\angle 4$ and $\angle 8$; alternate interior angles: $\angle 3$ and $\angle 6$, $\angle 4$ and $\angle 5$; alternate exterior angles: $\angle 1$ and $\angle 8$, $\angle 2$ and $\angle 7$; consecutive interior angles: $\angle 3$ and $\angle 5$, $\angle 4$ and $\angle 6$

b. $\angle 1$, $\angle 4$, $\angle 5$, and $\angle 8$ are congruent; $\angle 2$, $\angle 3$, $\angle 6$, and $\angle 7$ are congruent

c. 68 **d.** 27.5

e. yes; The situation described in part (c) meets this specification because $3 \cdot m\angle 3 = 3 \cdot 44° = 132° \leq m\angle 1 = 136° \leq 150°$. The situation described in part (d) does not meet this specification because $3 \cdot m\angle 3 = 3 \cdot 70° = 210° \nleq m\angle 1 = 110° \leq 150°$.

2. a. Complete answers should include an explanation that a transversal should be drawn on the graph and that one of the following theorems should be used along with measuring the appropriate angles to determine whether the lines are parallel: Corresponding Angles Converse (Thm. 3.5), Alternate Interior Angles Converse (Thm. 3.6), Alternate Exterior Angles Converse (Thm. 3.7), or Consecutive Interior Angles Converse (Thm. 3.8).

b. Complete answers should include a solution that shows a transversal drawn on the graph, the measures of the appropriate angles, and a statement of the theorem that was used.

c. The slopes of the lines should be determined and compared to determine whether they are equal.

d. The slope of each line is 4. Because the slopes are equal, the lines are parallel.

e. Complete answers should include measuring the appropriate angles to determine whether the lines are perpendicular and a reference to the Linear Pair Perpendicular Theorem (Thm. 3.10).

f. Complete answers should include measuring the appropriate angles and a statement of the Linear Pair Perpendicular Theorem (Thm. 3.10).

g. The slopes of the lines should be determined and multiplied to determine whether their product is -1.

h. The slope of ℓ is $-\frac{1}{4}$, and the slope of m is 4. Because the product of the slopes is -1, the lines are perpendicular.

Cumulative Test

1. $\overline{AB} \cong \overline{IJ}$; $\overline{OP} \cong \overline{LK} \cong \overline{EF}$; $\overline{CD} \cong \overline{GH} \cong \overline{MN}$

2. plane, line, point **3.** C

4. 19.06 units; 14 square units

5. rectangle; yes; The given rectangle has an area of 50 square units, which is $\frac{1}{25}$ of the required area, and a perimeter of 30 units, which is $\frac{1}{5}$ of the required perimeter. So, the given rectangle is $\frac{1}{5}$ of the size of the required swimming pool.

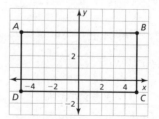

Answers

6. Step 1, a line segment was drawn longer than $\overline{AB}$. In step 2, the compass measured the length of $\overline{AB}$. In step 3, the compass was placed at C and marked point D on the new segment.

7. a. $\angle AGF$ and $\angle CGD$

   b. $\angle AGB$, $\angle DGB$, $\angle CGE$, and $\angle FGE$

   c. $\angle EGC$ and $\angle FGE$, $\angle AGB$ and $\angle DGB$, $\angle AGC$ and $\angle DGC$, $\angle CGD$ and $\angle FGD$

8. a. *Sample answer:* Through points D and E, there is exactly one line.

   b. *Sample answer:* The intersection of line ℓ and m is point C.

   c. *Sample answer:* Through points B, C, and F, there is exactly one plane, plane U.

   d. *Sample answer:* Point D and E lie in plane V, so $\overline{DE}$ lies in plane V.

   e. *Sample answer:* The intersection of plane U and plane V is line ℓ.

9. a. converse   b. contrapositive

   c. biconditional   d. inverse

10.

	STATEMENTS	REASONS
1.	$\overline{AB} \cong \overline{FE}$	1. Given
2.	$AB = FE$	2. Definition of congruent segments
3.	$\overline{AC} \cong \overline{FD}$	3. Given
4.	$AC = FD$	4. Definition of congruent segments
5.	$AB + BC = AC$	5. Segment Addition Postulate (Post. 1.2)
6.	$FE + BC = FD$	6. Substitution Property of Equality
7.	$BC = FD - FE$	7. Subtraction Property of Equality
8.	$FE + ED = FD$	8. Segment Addition Postulate (Post. 1.2)
9.	$ED = FD - FE$	9. Subtraction Property of Equality
10.	$BC = ED$	10. Substitution Property of Equality
11.	$\overline{BC} \cong \overline{ED}$	11. Definition of congruent segments

11. a. $3\sqrt{2}$ b. 6 c. $\sqrt{41}$ d. 7

    e. $\sqrt{82}$ f. $2\sqrt{2}$

    ordered from shortest to longest: f, a, b, c, d, e

12. In step 1, points A and B are equidistant from point P. In step 2, points A and B are equidistant from point Q. In step 3, where $\overleftrightarrow{PQ}$ intersects line m marks the shortest distance from either P or Q to line m.

13. a. $y = -\frac{1}{3}x$ b. $y = 3x - 14$

14. A, C, and D

15.

	STATEMENTS	REASONS
1.	$m \parallel n$	1. Given
2.	$\angle 1 \cong \angle 2$	2. Given
3.	$\angle 1 \cong \angle 4$	3. Vertical Angles Congruence Theorem (Thm. 2.6)
4.	$\angle 2 \cong \angle 3$	4. Vertical Angles Congruence Theorem (Thm. 2.6)
5.	$\angle 1 \cong \angle 3$	5. Substitution Property of Equality
6.	$\angle 3 \cong \angle 4$	6. Substitution Property of Equality

16. a. $(2, 8)$ b. 50 mi

Chapter 4

4.1–4.3 Quiz

1. 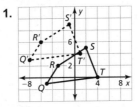   2.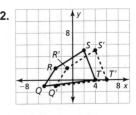

3. $\langle -7, 2 \rangle$ 4. $\langle -5, -11 \rangle$

5.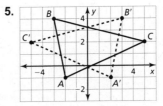

Answers

6.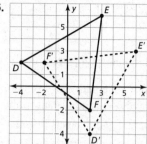

7. 1   **8.** 4

9. 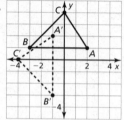   **10.**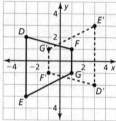

Test A

1. 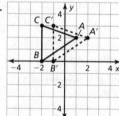   **2.**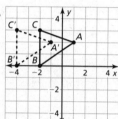

3. 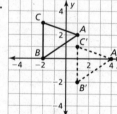   **4.**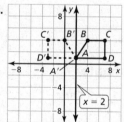

5.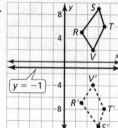

6. one horizontal line of symmetry.

7.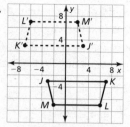

8. yes; A 180 degree rotation about the center maps the shape onto itself.

9. yes; A 90, 180, and 270 degrees rotation about the center will map the shape onto itself.

10. no

11. yes; $\triangle ABC$ can be mapped to $\triangle DEF$ by a translation 1 unit left and 5 units up, followed by a rotation 180° counterclockwise.

12. no; There is no rigid transformation which can map quadrilateral *JKLM* to quadrilateral *NOPQ*.

13. 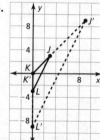   **14.**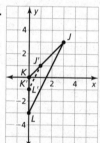

15. disagree; $m\angle C = 80°$ and that $m\angle E = 60°$, so the triangle are similar.

16. dilation scale factor: 2

17. dilation scale factor: $\frac{1}{2}$ and then reflection in the x-axis.

Test B

1. $A'(6, -2), B'(8, -2), C'(9, 1), D'(5, 1)$

2. $A'(3, 4), B'(4, 1), C'(3, -2), D'(2, 1)$

3. $(x, y) \rightarrow (x + 8, y - 3)$

4. $(x, y) \rightarrow (x - 2, y + 8)$

Answers

5.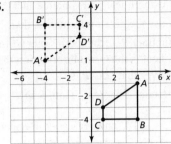

6.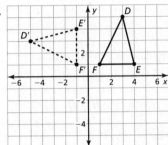

7. congruent; $\triangle ABC$ can be mapped to $\triangle EFG$ by a translation of 1 unit left and 2 units up.

8. similar; Quadrilateral $RSTU$ can be mapped to quadrilateral $MNOP$ by a dilation with a scale factor of 3, followed by a translation 3 units right and 8 units down.

9. line symmetry; no, rotational symmetry: yes; A 180° rotation about the center maps the figure onto itself.

10. line symmetry; yes, rotational symmetry: yes; The figure has line symmetry both horizontally and vertically through the center; A 180° rotation about the center maps the figure onto itself.

11. line symmetry; yes, rotational symmetry: no; The figure has line symmetry vertically down the center.

12. *Sample answer:* $(x, y) \rightarrow (x + 9, y)$, and then reflect in the x-axis

13. $(x, y) \rightarrow (x - 11, y)$, and then $(x, y) \rightarrow (x, y - 11)$

14. $k = 2.5$

15. $A'(-7, 17.5)$, $B'(3.5, 28)$, $C'(24.5, 17.5)$

16. $(x, y) \rightarrow \left(\frac{1}{3}x, \frac{1}{3}y\right)$

17. $(x, y) \rightarrow (x + 1, y - 5)$, and then $(x, y) \rightarrow (2x, 2y)$

Alternative Assessment

1. a. reflection: in the x-axis

b. translation $(x, y) \rightarrow (x - 2, y - 4)$

c. translation $(x, y) \rightarrow (x - 1, y + 1)$, dilation: $(x, y) \rightarrow (2x, 2y)$

d. rotation: 90 degrees counterclockwise about the origin

e. reflection: in the line $y = x$

f. translation: $(x, y) \rightarrow (x + 9, y)$, reflection: in the x-axis

2. a.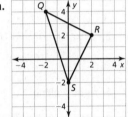

b. *Sample answer:* A rotation of 180 degrees counterclockwise about the origin, followed by a reflection in the x-axis, and then a reflection in the y-axis maps $\triangle QRS$ to its original position.

c. *Sample answer:* A dilation by a scale factor of $\frac{1}{2}$ followed by a translation 3 units right and 3 units down maps each vertex of $\triangle QRS$ to Quadrant IV.

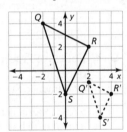

Chapter 5

5.1–5.4 Quiz

1. $x = 50°$; 50°   **2.** $x = 22$; 123°   **3.** $x = 15$; 151°

4. $\angle D \cong \angle L$, $\angle E \cong \angle M$, $\angle F \cong \angle N$;
$\overline{DE} \cong \overline{LM}$, $\overline{EF} \cong \overline{MN}$, $\overline{DF} \cong \overline{LN}$
Sample answer: $\triangle EFD \cong \triangle MNL$

5. $\angle A \cong \angle W$, $\angle B \cong \angle X$, $\angle C \cong \angle Y$, $\angle D \cong \angle Z$;
$\overline{AB} \cong \overline{WX}$, $\overline{BC} \cong \overline{XY}$, $\overline{CD} \cong \overline{YZ}$, $\overline{AD} \cong \overline{WZ}$
Sample answer: $CDAB \cong YZWX$

6. yes; $\overline{MK}$ is shared by both triangles, which provides the second congruent pair of sides.

Answers

7. yes; The angles between the two pairs of congruent sides are vertical angles, so they are congruent.

8. $\angle LMP \cong \angle LPM$; Base Angles Theorem (Thm. 5.6)

9. $\overline{NO} \cong \overline{MO}$; Converse of Base Angles Theorem (Thm. 5.7)

10. $\angle PMN \cong \angle PNM$; Base Angles Theorem (Thm. 5.6)

11. $x = 15,\ y = 49$ 12. $x = 61,\ y = 4$

13. $x = 11,\ y = 5$

Test A

1. $x = 26$; $52°$ and $128°$ 2. $x = 10$; $80°$ and $10°$

3. $x = 25$; $52°, 52°,$ and $76°$

4. obtuse isosceles   5. right scalene

6. $\overline{IW}$ 7. $\angle L$ 8. $\angle G$ 9. $92°$

10. $33°$ 11. $\triangle IGW$

12.

STATEMENTS	REASONS
1. $\overline{AB} \parallel \overline{CD}$	1. Given
2. $\overline{AB} \cong \overline{CD}$	2. Given
3. $\angle ABC \cong \angle DCB$	3. Alternate Interior Angles Theorem (Thm. 3.2)
4. $\overline{BC} \cong \overline{BC}$	4. Reflexive Property of Segment Congruence (Thm. 2.1)
5. $\triangle ABC \cong \triangle DCB$	5. SAS Congruence Theorem (Thm. 5.5)

13. $x = 4$ 14. $x = 8$

15. no; The known congruent angle is not between the two known congruent sides; to use the SAS Congruence Theorem (Thm. 5.5), you would need to know that either $\overline{FW} \cong \overline{YW}$ or $\angle FLW \cong \angle YLW$.

16. yes   17. yes

18. no; The triangles are similar, but there is not enough information given to establish congruence; to use the HL Congruence Theorem (Thm. 5.9), you would need to know that one of the angles is a right angle, and you would need information about the side lengths.

19. First, $\angle 2 \cong \angle 3$ using linear pairs and the fact that $\angle 1 \cong \angle 4$. Then use the given information that $CU = RS$ and subtract RU from both. This will leave $CR = US$. Last is the given information that $IC = IS$. This proves that $\angle CIR \cong \angle SIU$ by the SAS Congruence Theorem (Thm. 5.5).

20. $AB = \sqrt{13}$, $BC = \sqrt{13}$, and $AC = 4$; Because two sides are equal, that proves that $\triangle ABC$ is isosceles.

Test B

1. equilateral equiangular   2. scalene obtuse

3. isosceles obtuse

4. $x = 1.5$, $RQ = 3.9$, $RP = 3.9$, $PQ = 1.6$

5. $x = 9$, all side lengths $= 26$

6. $\angle W$ 7. $\overline{YZ}$ 8. $\overline{QR}$

9. $\angle R$ 10. $\overline{WZ}$ 11. $\angle Q$

12. $XWZY$ 13. $RQPS$

14. $x = 1$, $DE = 11$ 15. $55°$

16. $61°$ 17. $62.5°$ 18. $62.5°$

19. $55°$ 20. $75°$ 21. $50°$

22. yes; SAS Congruence Theorem (Thm. 5.5)

23. yes; HL Congruence Theorem (Thm. 5.9)

24. yes; AAS Congruence Theorem (Thm. 5.11)

25. no

26.

STATEMENTS	REASONS
1. $\overrightarrow{OM}$ bisects $\angle AOB$	1. Given
2. $\angle AOM \cong \angle BOM$	2. Definition of angle bisector
3. $\overrightarrow{MO}$ bisects $\angle AMB$	3. Given
4. $\angle AMO \cong \angle BMO$	4. Definition of angle bisector
5. $\overline{MO} \cong \overline{MO}$	5. Reflexive Property of Segment Congruence (Thm. 2.1)
6. $\triangle AMO \cong \triangle BMO$	6. ASA Congruence Theorem (Thm. 5.10)

Answers

27.

STATEMENTS	REASONS
1. $AB = AC$	1. Given
2. $\overline{AB} \cong \overline{AC}$	2. Definition of congruent segments
3. $\angle BAD \cong \angle CAD$	3. Given
4. $\overline{AD} \cong \overline{AD}$	4. Reflexive Property of Segment Congruence (Thm. 2.1)
5. $\triangle ABD \cong \triangle ACD$	5. SAS Congruence Theorem (Thm. 5.5)
6. $\overline{BD} \cong \overline{CD}$	6. Corresponding parts of congruent triangles are congruent
7. $BD = CD$	7. Definition of congruent segments

Alternative Assessment

1. a. right scalene; No sides are marked as congruent, and because $ABFE$ is a rectangle, $AB \neq AE$, so $\triangle ABE$ cannot be equilateral nor isosceles. So, $\triangle ABE$ is scalene. By measuring, $m\angle A = 90°$, $m\angle AEB = 50°$, and $m\angle ABE = 40°$. Because the triangle has a right angle, $\triangle ABE$ is a right triangle.

b. Side-Angle-Side (SAS) Congruence Theorem (Thm 5.5), Side-Side-Side (SSS) Congruence Theorem (Thm. 5.8), Hypotenuse-Leg (HL) Congruence Theorem (Thm. 5.9), Angle-Side-Angle (ASA) Congruence Theorem (Thm. 5.10), Angle-Angle-Side (AAS) Congruence Theorem (Thm. 5.11)

c. *Sample answers:*

Sample proof using Side-Angle-Side (SAS) Congruence Theorem:

Because $BCGF$ is a rectangle, $\overline{FB} \cong \overline{CG}$ and $\overline{BC} \cong \overline{GF}$. Also, because $BCGF$ is a rectangle, $m\angle FBC = m\angle CGF = 90°$. So, $\angle FBC \cong \angle CGF$ by the definition of congruent angles. By the SAS Congruence Theorem (Thm. 5.5), $\triangle FBC \cong \triangle CGF$.

Sample proof using Side-Side-Side (SSS) Congruence Theorem:

Because $BCGF$ is a rectangle, $\overline{FB} \cong \overline{CG}$ and $\overline{BC} \cong \overline{GF}$. By the Reflexive Property of Segment Congruence (Thm. 2.1), $\overline{CF} \cong \overline{CF}$. By the SSS Congruence Theorem (Thm. 5.8), $\triangle FBC \cong \triangle CGF$.

Sample proof using Hypotenuse-Leg (HL) Congruence Theorem:

Because $BCGF$ is a rectangle, $m\angle FBC = m\angle CGF = 90°$. So, $\triangle FBC$ and $\triangle CGF$ are right triangles by the definition of a right triangle. Also, because $BCGF$ is a rectangle, $\overline{FB} \cong \overline{CG}$. By the Reflexive Property of Segment Congruence (Thm. 2.1), $\overline{CF} \cong \overline{CF}$. By the HL Congruence Theorem (Thm. 5.9), $\triangle FBC \cong \triangle CGF$.

Sample proof using Angle-Side-Angle (ASA) Congruence Theorem:

Because $BCGF$ is a rectangle, $\overline{BF} \parallel \overline{CG}$. By the Alternate Interior Angles Theorem (Thm 3.2), $\angle BFC \cong \angle GCF$. Because $BCGF$ is a rectangle, $\overline{FB} \cong \overline{CG}$. Also, because $BCGF$ is a rectangle, $m\angle FBC = m\angle CGF = 90°$. So, $\angle FBC \cong \angle CGF$ by the definition of congruent angles. By the ASA Congruence Theorem (Thm. 5.10), $\triangle FBC \cong \triangle CGF$.

Sample proof using Angle-Angle-Side (AAS) Congruence Theorem:

Because $BCGF$ is a rectangle, $m\angle FBC = m\angle CGF = 90°$. So, $\angle FBC \cong \angle CGF$ by the definition of congruent angles. By the Alternate Interior Angles Theorem (Thm. 3.2.), $\angle BFC \cong \angle GCF$. By the Reflexive Property of Segment Congruence (Thm 2.1), $\overline{CF} \cong \overline{CF}$. By the AAS Congruence Theorem (Thm. 5.11), $\triangle FBC \cong \triangle CGF$.

Chapter 6

6.1–6.3 Quiz

1. 54   **2.** 22°

3. a. no

   b. no

4. a. yes

   b. yes

5. $(1.4, 2.6)$ **6.** $(3, 2)$ **7.** 45   **8.** 8

9. inside; $(4, 3)$

10. outside; $(-2, -3)$

11. always   **12.** never   **13.** sometimes

Answers

Test A

1. 10.2   2. 46   3. 93°   4. 34°

5. 46°, 16   6. $(6, -3)$

7. centroid is $(8, 0)$

8. $SM = 26$, $MR = 38$, and $UR = 57$

9. 8   10. 6   11. 6

12. yes; $4 + 7 > 10$ 13. no; $2 + 9 < 12$

14. no; Because $14 + 18 = 32$, this would be a flat line segment.

15. yes; $41.9 + 62.5 > 103$

16. $\angle J$, $\angle L$, $\angle K$ 17. $\angle L$, $\angle K$, $\angle J$

18. $TU > SV$ 19. $m\angle GHJ < m\angle KLM$

20. $AC < XZ$ 21. $\frac{1}{3} < x < 12$

22. $0 < x < 8$ 23. $3 < x < 7$

24. $m\angle QRP < m\angle SRP$ 25. $m\angle QPR > m\angle QRP$

26. $m\angle PRS < m\angle RSP$ 27. $m\angle RSP = m\angle RPS$

Test B

1. 16.2   2. 8   3. 16

4. 41°   5. 58°

6.
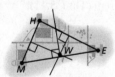

Check students' work. Students should find the circumcenter as shown.

7. 4   8. 28°   9. $(-1, 2)$

10. $(-4, 6)$ 11. $\left(-2, \frac{10}{3}\right)$

12. $(1, 2)$, $(2, -3)$, and $(5, 3)$

13. $(1, -1)$, $(-2, 4)$, and $(-5, -2)$

14. 6   15. 3   16. 2

17. 19 yd $< s <$ 29 yd

18. 5.5 in. $< s <$ 11.9 in.

19. 2.16 m $< s <$ 6.16 m

20. $\angle D$, $\angle F$, $\angle E$ 21. $\angle E$, $\angle F$, $\angle D$

22. $PS > RS$ 23. $m\angle BCA < m\angle DCA$

24. Assume $\triangle DEF$ has two obtuse angles. Let $\angle D$ and $\angle E$ be the obtuse angles. By the definition of an obtuse angle, $m\angle D > 90°$ and $m\angle E > 90°$.

If you add the inequalities, you obtain $m\angle D + m\angle E > 180°$. This is a contradiction of Triangle Sum Theorem (Thm. 5.1), which states $m\angle D + m\angle E + m\angle F = 180°$, because if $m\angle D + m\angle E > 180°$, then by substitution, $m\angle D + m\angle E = 180° - m\angle F$. This means that $180° - m\angle F > 180°$, so $m\angle F < 0°$. Because a triangle cannot have an angle with a measure less than $0°$, the assumption that a triangle can have more than one obtuse angle is false. So, a triangle can only have one obtuse angle.

Alternative Assessment

1. a. $(190, 48.18)$

b. $(100, 110)$, $(140, 110)$

c. 40 units

d. about $(130, 135)$

e. about $(33, 60)$

f. less than 7 ft

g. $\overline{BC}$; The shortest side is opposite the smallest angle.

h. circumcenter; The circumcenter is below the x-axis, so all portions of the gardens are within the view described.

Cumulative Test

1. C

2.
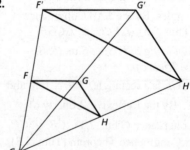

Answers

3.

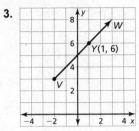

$Y(1, 6)$

4. a. *Sample answer:* translation
$(a, b) \rightarrow (a + 2, b)$ followed by rotation
$(a, b) \rightarrow (-a, -b)$

b. yes; Translations and rotations are rigid motions, so they preserve congruency.

5. A

6. $2, \frac{6}{5}, 3, \frac{5}{2}$

7. yes; *Sample answer:* The Triangle Sum Theorem (Thm. 5.1) states that the sum of the measures of the interior angles of a triangle is $180°$. So, the measures of the interior angles of both triangles in the Third Angles Theorem (Thm. 5.4) have a sum of $180°$. So, if the measures of two different sets of three angles add up to $180°$ and two pairs of angles are congruent, then the third pair is congruent as well.

8. In Step 2, $\overline{DE} \cong \overline{AB}$. In Step 3, $\overline{EF} \cong \overline{BC}$. In Step 4, $\overline{DF} \cong \overline{AC}$. So, $\triangle ABC \cong \triangle DEF$ by the SSS Congruence Theorem (Thm 5.8). If two triangles are congruent, then all their corresponding parts are congruent. So, $\angle EDF \cong \angle BAC$.

9. a. *Sample answer:* reflection $(a, b) \rightarrow (-a, b)$ followed by translation $(a, b) \rightarrow (a, b - 3)$

b. yes; $\angle A \cong \angle R$, $\angle B \cong \angle S$, $\angle C \cong \angle T$, $\overline{AB} \cong \overline{RS}$, $\overline{BC} \cong \overline{ST}$, $\overline{AC} \cong \overline{RT}$

10. a. *Sample answer:*

STATEMENTS	REASONS
1. $\overline{UV} \cong \overline{YZ}$	1. Given
2. $\angle U \cong \angle Y$	2. Given
3. $TU = 3$	3. Distance Formula
4. $XY = 3$	4. Distance Formula
5. $TU = XY$	5. Substitution Property of Equality
6. $\overline{TU} \cong \overline{XY}$	6. Definition of congruent sides
7. $\triangle TUV \cong \triangle XYZ$	7. SAS Congruence Theorem (Thm. 5.5)

b. *Sample answer:*
Rotation $(a, b) \rightarrow (b, -a)$ followed by translation $(a, b) \rightarrow (a + 4, b + 8)$

11. A, B, C

12. Use the Distance Formula to find AB and AC, the lengths of two sides of the triangle.

$$AB = \sqrt{(5 - 3)^2 + (7 - 3)^2}$$
$$= \sqrt{2^2 + 4^2}$$
$$= \sqrt{4 + 16}$$
$$= \sqrt{20}$$
$$= 2\sqrt{5}$$

$$AC = \sqrt{(7 - 5)^2 + (7 - 3)^2}$$
$$= \sqrt{2^2 + 4^2}$$
$$= \sqrt{4 + 16}$$
$$= \sqrt{20}$$
$$= 2\sqrt{5}$$

So, $AB = AC$. By the definition of an isosceles triangle, $\triangle ABC$ is an isosceles triangle.

13. *Sample answers:* Angle Addition Postulate (Post. 1.4); Substitution Property of Equality; Triangle Larger Angle Theorem (Thm. 6.10); Triangle Longer Side Theorem (Thm. 6.9); Segment Addition Postulate (Post. 1.2)

Answers

14.

STATEMENTS	REASONS
1. $\overline{BD}$ is the perpendicular bisector of $\overline{AC}$	1. Given
2. $\overline{AD} \cong \overline{DC}$	2. Definition of perpendicular bisector
3. $\angle BDA$ is a right angle; $\angle BDC$ is a right angle	3. Definition of perpendicular lines
4. $\angle BDA \cong \angle BDC$	4. Right Angles Congruence Theorem (Them. 2.3)
5. $\overline{BD} \cong \overline{BD}$	5. Reflexive Property of Segment Congruence (Thm. 2.1)
6. $\triangle BAD \cong \triangle BCD$	6. SAS Congruence Theorem (Thm. 5.5)
7. $\overline{BA} \cong \overline{BC}$	7. Corresponding parts of congruent triangles are congruent

15. B

16. a. $(6, 6)$

   b. $y = -2x + 18$

17. yes; Reflections and dilations are similarity transformations because they do not change the angles and they preserve the ratio of the sides.

18. The slope of AC is 1, and the slope of $A'C'$ is 1.

Chapter 7

7.1–7.3 Quiz

1. $720°$ **2.** $2700°$ **3.** $3960°$

4. 56   **5.** 30

6. interior: $140°$, exterior: $40°$

7. interior: $165.6°$, exterior: $14.4°$

8. 11.7   **9.** 8.5   **10.** $113°$ **11.** $115°$

12. $35°$ **13.** $78°$

14. Parallelogram Opposite Sides Converse Theorem (Thm. 7.7); If both pairs of opposite sides of a quadrilateral are congruent, then the quadrilateral is a parallelogram.

15. Parallelogram Diagonals Converse Theorem (Thm. 7.10); If the diagonals of a quadrilateral bisect each other, then the quadrilateral is a parallelogram.

Test A

1. interior: $540°$, exterior: $360°$

2. interior: $360°$, exterior: $360°$

3. interior: $1800°$, exterior: $360°$

4. 100   **5.** 120   **6.** $11.25°$ **7.** $360°$

8. 23; The Parallelogram Opposite Sides Theorem (Thm. 7.3) states if a quadrilateral is a parallelogram, then its opposite sides are congruent. So, $x + 21 = 12x - 1$, and $x = 2$. So, $AD = 23$.

9. $63°$; The Parallelogram Consecutive Angles Theorem (Thm. 7.5) states that if a quadrilateral is a parallelogram, then its consecutive angles are supplementary. So, $y - 9 + \left(\dfrac{y}{2}\right) = 180$, and $y = 126$. So, $m\angle D = 63°$, and by the Parallelogram Opposite Angles Theorem (Thm. 7.4), $m\angle B = 63°$.

10. $G(-5, -7)$

11. 123.8 cm; Parallelogram Opposite Sides Theorem (Thm. 7.3)

12. 108.8 cm; Parallelogram Diagonals Theorem (Thm. 7.6)

13. $123°$; Parallelogram Consecutive Angles Theorem (Thm. 7.5)

14. $123°$; Parallelogram Opposite Angles Theorem (Thm. 7.4)

15. 217.6 cm; Parallelogram Diagonals Theorem (Thm. 7.6)

16. $57°$; Parallelogram Opposite Angles Theorem (Thm. 7.4)

17. $x = 23$, $y = 20$ **18.** $x = 4$, $y = 7$

19. *Sample answer:* $\overline{BD}$ and $\overline{FH}$ have the same slope $\frac{1}{5}$, and $\overline{BH}$ and $\overline{FD}$ have the same slope -6. So, $BD \parallel FH$ and $BH \parallel FD$.

20. rhombus; by the Rhombus Corollary (Cor. 7.2)

Answers

21. rectangle; Rectangle Diagonals Theorem (Thm. 7.13)

22. square; By the Rhombus Corollary (Cor. 7.2), it is a rhombus, and by the Rectangle Corollary (Cor. 7.3), it is a rectangle. A rectangle that is also a rhombus is a square.

23. 20°   **24.** 140°   **25.** 8

26. yes; no   **27.** no

28. 17   **29.** 27   **30.** 138°   **31.** 52°

Test B

1. 56°   **2.** 128°   **3.** 100°   **4.** 76°

5. 150°   **6.** 22.5°   **7.** 8   **8.** 136°

9. $x = 15$, $y = 12$ **10.** $x = 7$, $y = 4$

11. Parallelogram Opposite Sides Converse (Thm. 7.7); If both pairs of opposite sides of a quadrilateral are congruent, then the quadrilateral is a parallelogram.

12. Parallelogram Opposite Angles Converse (Thm. 7.8); By the Polygon Interior Angles Theorem (Thm. 7.1), $m\angle R = 120° = m\angle T$. If both pairs of opposite angles are congruent, then the quadrilateral is a parallelogram.

13. yes; The diagonals of the quadrilateral bisect each other.

14. no; You are only given the four angles where the diagonals intersect. None of the conditions are met, so it is not a parallelogram.

15. yes; One angle is supplementary to both its consecutive angles.

16. square; All four angles are congruent and all four sides are congruent.

17. rectangle; All four angles are congruent, but each side is only congruent to its opposite side.

18. rhombus; It is a parallelogram because its consecutive angles are supplementary, and it is a rhombus because all its sides are congruent.

19. 46.2   **20.** 41   **21.** 92.4   **22.** 46.2

23. rectangle, square, and rhombus; All four sides are congruent and all four angles are congruent.

24. rhombus; All four sides are congruent, but all four angles are not congruent.

25. 71°   **26.** 15°   **27.** 71°   **28.** 30°

29. 124   **30.** 19

Alternative Assessment

1. *Sample answer:*

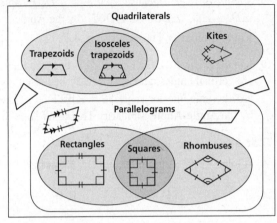

2. a. 144°

  b. $\overline{AB} \cong \overline{CB}$, $\overline{AD} \cong \overline{CD}$, $\angle A \cong \angle C$

  c. *Sample answer:* EFGH is a rhombus and a parallelogram. The diagonals $\overline{EG}$ and $\overline{FH}$ are perpendicular and bisect each other. $\overline{EH} \parallel \overline{FG}$, $\overline{EF} \parallel \overline{HG}$, $\overline{EH} \cong \overline{FG}$, $\overline{EF} \cong \overline{HG}$, $\angle E \cong \angle G$, and $\angle F \cong \angle H$.

  d. $m\angle F = 131°$; Because $\angle E$ and $\angle F$ are consecutive angles in a parallelogram, they are supplementary by the Parallelogram Consecutive Angles Theorem (Thm. 7.5).

  e. $TW = 5.5$ mm; $RY = 10.5$ mm

  f. *Sample answer:* Measure the opposite sides of the facet's polygon shape to show that they are congruent.

Chapter 8

8.1–8.2 Quiz

1. $\angle L \cong \angle A$, $\angle N \cong \angle B$, $\angle M \cong \angle C$;
$$\frac{AB}{LN} = \frac{BC}{NM} = \frac{CA}{ML}$$

2. $\angle D \cong \angle M$, $\angle E \cong \angle N$, $\angle F \cong \angle O$, $\angle G \cong \angle P$;
$$\frac{DE}{MN} = \frac{EF}{MO} = \frac{EG}{OP} = \frac{GD}{PM}$$

3. 21   **4.** 19.5

5. The ratio of the perimeter of *ABCD* to the perimeter of *WXYZ* is $\frac{2}{5}$.

Answers

6. The ratio of the perimeter of *ABCD* to the perimeter of *WXYZ* is $\frac{4}{1}$.

7. no   **8.** yes, *HIJK* ≅ *QRST*

9. *Sample answer:* Because ∠*DEF* ≅ ∠*DGH* and ∠*D* ≅ ∠*D*, △*DEF* ~ △*DGH* by the Angle-Angle Similarity Theorem (Thm. 8.3).

10. *Sample answer:* ∠*WXV* ≅ ∠*ZXY* because they are vertical angles, and ∠*V* ≅ ∠*Z*, because they are alternate interior angles. So, ∠*WXV* ~ ∠*YXZ* by the Angle-Angle Similarity Theorem (Thm. 8.3).

Test A

1. similar   **2.** similar   **3.** similar

4. $\frac{3}{2}$ **5.** 16   **6.** 9

7. ∠*L*   **8.** ∠*Q*   **9.** *PQ*   **10.** 11

11. yes; △*ABC* ~△*DEF*; The missing angle of △*ABC* is 41°, so the AA Similarity Theorem (Thm. 8.3) applies.

12. no; The ratios of corresponding sides are not equal.

13. no; There is only one congruent angle.

14. 15 ft   **15.** 5   **16.** 12

17. 6   **18.** 30   **19.** $8\frac{2}{3}$

20. 10   **21.** 2.4   **22.** 7

23. 4.8   **24.** 11   **25.** 13.2   **26.** 22

Test B

1. 20   **2.** 10   **3.** 8

4. $\frac{6}{5}$; ∠*C* ≅ ∠*D*, ∠*A* ≅ ∠*F*, ∠*B* ≅ ∠*E*;

$$\frac{AC}{DF} = \frac{BC}{DE} = \frac{AB}{EF}$$

5. $\frac{2}{5}$; ∠*A* ≅ ∠*E*, ∠*B* ≅ ∠*F*, ∠*C* ≅ ∠*G*,

∠*D* ≅ ∠*H*; $\frac{AB}{EF} = \frac{BC}{FG} = \frac{AD}{EH} = \frac{DC}{GH}$

6. 133.64 mi   **7.** 28 ft

8. *Sample answer:* It is given that ∠*BAC* ≅ ∠*EDC*, and ∠*BCA* ≅ ∠*ECD* by the Vertical Angles Congruence Theorem (Thm. 2.6). So, △*BAC* ~ △*EDC* by the AA Similarity Theorem (Thm. 8.3); △*BAC* ~ △*EDC*

9. *Sample answer:* Because $\frac{BC}{AC} = \frac{EC}{DC}$ and ∠*BCA* ≅ ∠*ECD* by the Vertical Angles Congruence Theorem (Thm. 2.6), △*BAC* ~ △*EDC* by the SAS Similarity Theorem (Thm. 8.5); △*BAC* ~ △*EDC*

10. no; Based on this information, the triangles are not similar because the sides are not all proportional.

11. no; Although the proportion $\frac{ED}{DC} = \frac{AB}{BC}$ is true, there is not enough information given to determine whether ∠*ABC* ≅ ∠*CDE*.

12. 9   **13.** 15   **14.** 6

15. 14 ft   **16.** 14.4 ft   **17.** *AG*

18. *DE*   **19.** *FE*   **20.** *GC*

21. 6   **22.** 11.2   **23.** 4.5   **24.** 150 yd

Alternative Assessment

1. a. $\frac{AH}{DH} = \frac{60 + 60}{60} = \frac{2}{1}$,

$\frac{BH}{EH} = \frac{BE + EH}{EH} = \frac{EH + EH}{EH} = \frac{2}{1}$, and

∠*H* ≅ ∠*H*. So, △*ABH* ~ △*DEH* by the SAS Similarity Theorem (Thm. 8.5).

b. 7 in.; *Sample answer:* From part (a) △*ABH* ~ △*DEH*, so the side lengths are proportional, $\frac{120}{60} = \frac{14}{DE}$.

c. *Sample answer:* Because they are corresponding parts of similar triangles, ∠*ABE* ≅ ∠*DEH*, so $\overline{AC} \parallel \overline{DG}$ by the Corresponding Angles Converse (Thm. 3.5).

d. *Sample answer:* ∠*ACI* ≅ ∠*EFI* by the Corresponding Angles Theorem (Thm. 3.1), and ∠*CIA* ≅ ∠*FIE* by the Reflexive Property of Angle Congruence (Thm 2.2.). So, △*ACI* ~ △*EFI* by the AA Similarity Theorem (Thm. 8.3).

Answers

e. 2468 in.^{2}; *Sample answer:* Because $AH = 120$ and $DH = 60$, the sides have a ratio of $\frac{2}{1}$ and the areas have a ratio of $\left(\frac{2}{1}\right)^2 = \frac{4}{1}$.

f. at least 4 in.; *Sample answer:* The ratio of side lengths of $ABED$ to $ACIH$ is 1 to 2, so $AC = 28$. The vertical distance between the ramp surface and $\overline{AH}$ must be at least 4 inches for the ramp to be at least 32 inches high.

2. $TU = 20$ ft; The 30-foot side is twice the length of the 15-foot side in $\triangle STU$, and $\overline{XZ}$ is twice as long as $\overline{XY}$ in $\triangle XYZ$. So, $\overline{YZ}$ corresponds to the third side $\overline{TU}$ of $\triangle STU$. This gives the proportional relationship $\dfrac{12}{15} = \dfrac{24}{30} = \dfrac{16}{TU}$.

Chapter 9

9.1–9.3 Quiz

1. 12; yes   **2.** $\sqrt{65}$; no   **3.** 8; yes

4. 192 cm^2 **5.** 168 m^2 **6.** obtuse

7. acute   **8.** right

9. $x = 5\sqrt{2}$, $y = 5$ **10.** $x = 8\sqrt{3}$, $y = 8$

11. $x = 3\sqrt{3}$, $y = 6\sqrt{3}$

12. 6   **13.** 24   **14.** $3\sqrt{7}$

15. $\triangle CAB \cong \triangle CDA \cong \triangle ADB$; $x = 2\sqrt{5}$

16. $\triangle FED \cong \triangle FGE \cong \triangle EGD$; $x = 6\sqrt{6}$

Test A

1. $\sqrt{29}$; no   **2.** $2\sqrt{5}$; no   **3.** 7; yes

4. no   **5.** yes; acute   **6.** no

7. yes; right   **8.** about 596.3 m

9. $x = 4$, $y = 2\sqrt{2}$ **10.** $x = 8\sqrt{3}$, $y = 8$

11. $x = 5\sqrt{3}$, $y = 5$

12. $\triangle CBD \sim \triangle ABC \sim \triangle ACD$; $x = 100$

13. $\triangle BCA \sim \triangle DCB \sim \triangle DBA$; $x = 48$

14. $\triangle BAC \sim \triangle BCD \sim \triangle CAD$; $x = 15$

15. $10\sqrt{3}$ **16.** $6\sqrt{2}$ **17.** 6

18. $\tan A = \frac{7}{24} \approx 0.29$, $\tan B = \frac{24}{7} \approx 3.43$

19. $\tan A = \frac{5}{12} \approx 0.42$, $\tan B = \frac{12}{5} = 2.4$

20. $\tan A = \frac{3}{4} = 0.75$, $\tan B = \frac{4}{3} \approx 1.33$

21. 12.9   **22.** 10.8   **23.** 14.6

24. $\frac{8}{17} \approx 0.47$ **25.** $\frac{15}{17} \approx 0.88$ **26.** $\frac{15}{17} \approx 0.88$

27. $\frac{8}{17} \approx 0.47$ **28.** 9.6°   **29.** about 23.5 ft

30. 82.2°

Test B

1. 24; yes   **2.** 41; yes   **3.** $4\sqrt{21}$; no

4. acute; The triangle formed contains all acute triangles.

5. $10\sqrt{2}$ **6.** 8   **7.** $8\sqrt{3}$

8. $x = 100\sqrt{2} \approx 141.4$ ft

9. $x = 4$, $y = 2\sqrt{13}$ **10.** $x = 18$, $y = 6\sqrt{10}$

11. $x = 18$, $y = 24$ **12.** $\tan A = \frac{3}{5} = 0.6$

13. $\tan B = \frac{5}{3} \approx 1.7$

14. 31°   **15.** 59°   **16.** about 86.9 ft

17. about 17.5 ft   **18.** $\frac{12}{37} \approx 0.32$ **19.** $\frac{35}{37} \approx 0.95$

20. $\frac{35}{37} \approx 0.95$ **21.** $\frac{12}{37} \approx 0.32$

22. $x = 14.6$, $y = 8.8$ **23.** $x = 12.4$, $y = 15.9$

24. $x = 23.8$, $y = 31.1$

Alternative Assessment

1. a. 8 ft; *Sample answer:* Using the Pythagorean Theorem (Thm. 9.1), half the distance is $\sqrt{5^2 - 3^2} = 4$ feet.

b. obtuse; *Sample answer:* Because $8^2 > 5^2 + 5^2$, the triangle is obtuse.

Copyright © Big Ideas Learning, LLC
All rights reserved.

Geometry   **A19**
Answers

Answers

c. $106.3°$

d. 4.6 ft

e. 9.2 ft

f. 4 ft

g. $\sin 60° = \dfrac{\sqrt{3}}{2}$, $\cos 60° = \dfrac{1}{2}$, $\tan 60° = \sqrt{3}$

h. *Sample answer:* first design; second design; The first design is more convenient for heating up leftovers because there is less distance between the refrigerator and the stove; The second design is more convenient for cleaning up because there is less distance between the stove and the sink.

2. a. To find $m\angle A$ given all three side lengths, use the Law of Cosines.

b. To find $m\angle A$ given $m\angle B$ and the lengths of sides a and b, use the Law of Sines.

Cumulative Test

1.

STATEMENTS	REASONS
1. *ABCD* and *GDEF* are parallelograms.	**1.** Given
2. $\angle CDA \cong \angle EDG$	**2.** Vertical Angles Congruence Theorem (Thm. 2.6)
3. $m\angle CDA + m\angle A = 180°$	**3.** Parallelogram Consecutive Angles Theorem (Thm. 7.5)
4. $m\angle EDG + m\angle G = 180°$	**4.** Parallelogram Consecutive Angles Theorem (Thm. 7.5)
5. $m\angle CDA + m\angle A = m\angle EDG + m\angle G$	**5.** Substitution
6. $m\angle CDA = m\angle EDG$	**6.** Definition of congruence
7. $m\angle CDA + m\angle A = m\angle CDA + m\angle G$	**7.** Substitution
8. $m\angle A = m\angle G$	**8.** Subtraction Property of Equality
9. $\angle A \cong \angle G$	**9.** Definition of congruence

2. $6\sqrt{13} \approx 21.6$ units; yes; no; no; equilateral because all sides have the same length; not equiangular because the angles are not all the same; not regular because not equiangular

3. Step 1: >; >

Step 2: =; >; >; >

Step 3: =

4.

STATEMENTS	REASONS
1. *ABCD* is a rectangle. *BCED* is a parallelogram.	**1.** Given
2. $\overline{BD} \cong \overline{CE}$	**2.** Parallelogram Opposite Sides Theorem (Thm. 7.3)
3. $\overline{BD} \cong \overline{AC}$	**3.** Rectangle Diagonals Theorem (Thm. 7.13)
4. $\overline{AC} \cong \overline{CE}$	**4.** Substitution
5. $\triangle ACE$ is an isosceles triangle.	**5.** Definition of isosceles triangle

5. a. $(x, y) \rightarrow \left(\frac{1}{2}x, \frac{1}{2}y\right)$

$(x, y) \rightarrow (-x, y)$

b. yes; Dilations and reflections are similarity transformations that preserve angle measure.

6. SAS Congruence Theorem (Thm. 5.5)

7. *Sample answer:* $BC = 3$ and $CD = 4$; $BC = 1.5$ and $CD = 2$; $BC = 2$ and $CD = \frac{8}{3}$

8. B, C

9. yes; $\dfrac{AB + BC + AC}{JK + KL + JL} = 3$;

$\dfrac{AB}{JK} = \dfrac{BC}{KL} = \dfrac{AC}{JL} = 3$;

$(a, b) \rightarrow \left(-\frac{1}{3}a, -\frac{1}{3}b\right)$

10. rectangle

11. $\dfrac{DE}{TU} = \dfrac{EF}{UV} = \dfrac{FG}{VW} = \dfrac{DG}{TW} = k$;

$\dfrac{\text{area of } DEFG}{\text{area of } TUVW} = k^2$

12. C

13. $m\angle J = 90°$

Answers

14. $\sin A \boxed{>} \sin F$; $\sin A \boxed{=} \cos C$; $\cos C \boxed{=} \cos F$; $\tan C \boxed{<} \tan D$; $\cos D \boxed{<} \cos F$; $\sin C \boxed{=} \sin F$

15. 971 in.

16. *Sample answer:* $\sin P = \dfrac{\sqrt{2}}{2}$; $\cos P = \dfrac{\sqrt{2}}{2}$;

$\sin P = \cos P$; $\tan P = 1$; $\dfrac{PQ}{PR} = \dfrac{\sqrt{2}}{2}$;

$\cos P = \dfrac{PQ}{PR}$; $\sin R = \dfrac{PQ}{PR}$; $\sin R = \cos R$;

$\tan R = 1$; $\tan R = \tan P$

17. C

Chapter 10

10.1–10.3 Quiz

1. $\odot C$

2. $\overline{BA}$

3. *Sample answer:* $\overline{CA}$

4. $\overline{AE}$

5. *Sample answer:* $\overline{AF}$

6. $\overline{DE}$

7. 10

8. 5

9. minor arc; 110°

10. major arc; 243°

11. semicircle; 180°

12. minor arc; 117°

13. yes; $m\angle HOJ = m\angle IOK$ by definition of vertical angles. So $m\overset{\frown}{HJ} = m\overset{\frown}{KI}$ by the Congruent Central Angles Theorem (Thm. 10.4).

14. no; $\overset{\frown}{LN}$ and $\overset{\frown}{MO}$ have the same measure but are not congruent because they are arcs of circles that are not congruent.

15. 273°

Test A

1. diameter

2. radius

3. secant

4. tangent

5. radius

6. chord

7. 5

8. 16

9. 4

10. no; $\triangle EFG$ is not a right triangle, so $\overline{FG}$ is not tangent to $\odot E$.

11. 155°

12. 108°

13. 240°

14. 220

15. $x = 134$, $y = 75$

16. $x = 75$, $y = 150$

17. 33

18. 15

19. 8

20. center: $(1, -3)$, radius: 2

21. center: $(2, 1)$, radius: 4

22. center: $(0, 3)$, radius: $\sqrt{14}$

23. center: $(1, -4)$, radius: 3

24. $(x - 1)^2 + (y - 2)^2 = 25$

25. $(x + 3)^2 + (y - 5)^2 = 4$

26. $(x - 2)^2 + (y - 4)^2 = 16$

27. $(x + 1)^2 + (y + 4)^2 = 9$

Test B

1. $\overline{BE}$

2. $\overline{AH}$

3. line ℓ

4. *Sample answer:* $\overline{FC}$

5. *Sample answer:* Point A

6. $\overline{BI}$

7. 12

8. 74

9. 20

10. 19.9 cm

11. 28 ft

12. 3

13. 122°

14. $x = 15$, $y = 0$

15. 2

16. 3

17. 4

18. 70

19. 109°

20. 200°

21. $(x - 6)^2 + (y + 12)^2 = 6400$

22. no

23. yes

24. $(x + 5)^2 + (y - 4)^2 = 4$

25. $(x - 10)^2 + (y + 2)^2 = 36$

26. $(x - 11)^2 + (y + 8)^2 = 74$

27. $(x + 4)^2 + (y - 6)^2 = 16$

28. $(x - 6)^2 + (y - 8)^2 = 65$

Answers

Alternative Assessment

1. If two chords intersect inside a circle, then the measure of each angle is one-half the sum of the measures of the arcs intercepted by the angle and its vertical angle. If two lines intersect outside a circle and both lines intersect the circle, then the measure of the angle formed is one-half the difference of the measures of the intercepted arcs. The measure of an inscribed angle is one-half the measure of its intercepted arc. If a tangent and a chord intersect at a point on a circle, then the measures of each angle formed is one-half the measure of its intercepted arc.

2. **a.** $\overline{AB}$, $\overline{AD}$, $\overline{BE}$, $\overline{CG}$, $\overline{DE}$, and $\overline{FH}$ are chords; $\overline{AD}$ and $\overline{BE}$ are diameters; $\overline{OA}$, $\overline{OB}$, $\overline{OD}$, $\overline{OE}$, and $\overline{OH}$ are radii.

   b. $m\overarc{EFH} = 131°$; $m\overarc{ECH} = 229°$

   c. $20°$

   d. $108°$

   e. $CG = 40$, $FH = 26$

   f. no; The equation of the circle is $x^2 + y^2 = 441$. $(14, 17)$ is not a solution, because $14^2 + 17^2 = 196 + 289 = 485 \neq 441$.

Chapter 11

11.1–11.4 Quiz

1. about $75.3°$

2. about 40.1 km

3. about 62.8 cm

4. $\dfrac{4\pi}{3}$

5. $130°$

6. 14.1 cm^2

7. 102.6 in^2

8. O

9. *Sample answer:* $\overline{AO}$ 10. $\overline{OP}$

11. *Sample answer:* $\angle BOA$

12. $m\angle BOA = 60°$, $m\angle AOP = 30°$, and $m\angle PAO = 60°$

13. $96\sqrt{3} \approx 166.28$ square units

14. yes; pentagonal prism   15. no

16. yes; rectangular pyramid

Test A

1. about 22.92 in.

2. about 6.11 cm

3. about $137°$

4. $\dfrac{\pi}{3}$

5. $\dfrac{17\pi}{9}$

6. $-\pi$

7. $345°$

8. $300°$

9. $195°$

10. about 8.55 in.^{2}

11. about 255.69 cm^2

12. both regions' area is about 139.63 in.^{2}

13. about 13.73 in.^{2}

14. about 10.27 m^2

15. about 30.90 in.^{2}

16. about 141.3 ft^2

17. 97.5 square units

18. 75 square units

19. about 623.23 square units

20. about 549.8 in.^{3}

21. 48 cm^3

22. about 997.66 ft^3

23. $2{,}592{,}100$ m^3

24. about 44.32 in.^{3}

25. about 18.88 in.^{2}

Test B

1. 189 ft

2. 1047 ft

3. 83.17 units

4. $83.1°$

5. $-\dfrac{\pi}{4}$

6. $108°$

7. $\dfrac{13\pi}{9}$

8. 15.7 cm^2

9. about 31.42 ft^2

10. about 3.27 ft^2

11. 72 cm^2

12. 50 m^2

13. 160 cm^2

14. 6 m

15. 12 in.

16. 1920 square units

17. about 209.6 square units

18. 1602.3 square units

Answers

19.

The solid has a circular base. It is a cylinder.

20.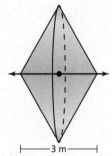

The solid is made up of two cones.

21. Box A; It has the greatest volume (5760 cubic inches).

22. 37,373,067 ft^3 **23.** 128,177 mm^3

24. 13,195 mm^2

Alternative Assessment

1. a. $931\pi \approx 2924.82$ in.^{3}; 4500 in.^{3}

b. $6.125\pi \approx 19.24$ in.^{2}; Because the sector has an intercepted arc of $\dfrac{\pi}{4} = 45°$, its area is one-eighth of the area of the circular drum head. So, divide the area of the drum head by 8.

c. 12 ft^3

d. 384 cm^3; yes; The given edge lengths can be used to find the areas of two of the faces, and the Pythagorean Theorem (Thm. 9.1) can be used to find the additional edge lengths needed to find the areas of the other two faces.

e. 1060 cm^3

f. 459.5 cm^2

g. $150\sqrt{3} \approx 259.81$ in.^{2}; Use formula $A = \frac{1}{2}aP$, where $P = 60$ inches is the perimeter of the regular hexagon with side lengths of 10 inches, and $a = 5\sqrt{3}$ inches is the apothem, which is the length of the longer leg of a 30°-60°-90° triangle whose shorter leg is 5 inches long.

h. 2272 in.^{3}

Chapter 12

12.1–12.3 Quiz

1. $\frac{3}{5}$ **2.** 0.47   **3.** $\frac{3}{7}$

4. 0.98   **5.** $\frac{1}{6}, \frac{6}{25}$ **6.** $0.2\overline{6}$

7. 0.175

8. a. 0.0156

b. 0.96

c. 0.0286

9. probability that the person chooses the first benefit package = 0.45; probability that the person chooses the second benefit package = 0.55; probability that the person is a man = 0.4; probability that the person is a woman = 0.6

Test A

1. $\frac{1}{6}$ **2.** $\frac{1}{2}$ **3.** $\frac{1}{2}$

4. 0   **5.** 10   **6.** 210

7. 70   **8.** 1680   **9.** Company 1

10. no; If A and B were independent events, then $P(A) \bullet P(B) = \frac{3}{14} \bullet \frac{1}{5} = \frac{3}{70}$, not $\frac{3}{65}$.

11. a. about 50.27%

b. about 49.73%

c. about 12.7%

12. a.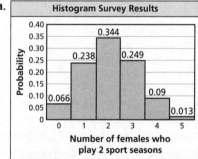

b. 2 of the 5 female students will play 2 sport seasons

c. about 35.2%

13. a. $\frac{7}{13}$ **b.** $\frac{12}{221}$

14. a. $\frac{1}{455}$ **b.** $\frac{1}{2730}$

Answers

1. $\frac{1}{8}$ **2.** $\frac{3}{8}$ **3.** $\frac{1}{2}$

4. 0   **5.** 95,040   **6.** 35

7. 1716   **8.** 3024   **9.** Book Class

10. yes; Switching the event names A and B in the text formula $P(A \text{ and } B) = P(A) \bullet P(B \mid A)$ gives the formula $P(B \text{ and } A) = P(B) \bullet P(A \mid B)$. But $P(B \text{ and } A) = P(A \text{ and } B)$, so the given formula is in fact equivalent to the formula stated in the text.

11. a. 10%

     b. 90%

     c. 0.1%

12. a.

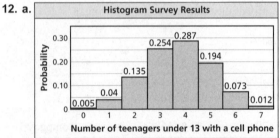

     b. 4 teenagers under the age of 13 will own a cell phone

     c. about 56.6%

13. a. $\frac{5}{21}$

     b. $\frac{10}{147}$

     c. $\frac{1}{21}$

14. a. $\frac{1}{1140}$

     b. $\frac{1}{6840}$

Alternative Assessment

1. a. odd; *Sample answer:* There are 5 odd spaces and 4 even. The probability of landing on an odd is $\frac{5}{9}$ and the probability of landing on an even is $\frac{4}{9}$. But this does not mean you are more likely to win the game because the game is based on the product of two spins, not just one spin.

     b. independent; The second spin is not affected by the first.

     c. There are 81 possible outcomes.

d. (1, 1), (1, 2), (1, 3), (1, 4), (1, 5), (1, 6), (1, 7), (1, 8), (1, 9), (2, 1), (2, 2), (2, 3), (2, 4), (2, 5), (2, 6), (2, 7) (2, 8), (2, 9), (3, 1), (3, 2), (3, 3), (3, 4), (3, 5), (3, 6), (3, 7), (3, 8), (3, 9), (4, 1), (4, 2), (4, 3), (4, 4), (4, 5), (4, 6), (4, 7), (4, 8), (4, 9), (5, 1), (5, 2), (5, 3), (5, 4), (5, 5), (5, 6), (5, 7), (5, 8), (5, 9), (6, 1), (6, 2), (6, 3), (6, 4), (6, 5), (6, 6), (6, 7), (6, 8), (6, 9), (7, 1), (7, 2), (7, 3), (7, 4), (7, 5), (7, 6), (7, 7), (7, 8), (7, 9), (8, 1), (8, 2), (8, 3), (8, 4), (8, 5), (8, 6), (8, 7), (8, 8), (8, 9), (9, 1), (9, 2), (9, 3), (9, 4) (9, 5), (9, 6), (9, 7), (9, 8), (9, 9)

e. $\frac{25}{81}$

f. $\frac{56}{81}$

g. no; *Sample answer:* You lose if the product of the two numbers is even, and you are more than twice as likely to have an even product than an odd product.

h. One spin must be a prime number and the other must be 1.

i. *Sample answer:* The probability of the first described turn is $\frac{1}{9} \bullet \frac{5}{9} = \frac{5}{81}$. So, $P(\text{Turn 1}) = \frac{5}{81}$; The probability of the second described turn is $\frac{5}{9} \bullet \frac{1}{9} = \frac{5}{81}$. So, $P(\text{Turn 2}) = \frac{5}{81}$. Then $P(\text{Turn 1 or Turn 2}) = \frac{5}{81} + \frac{5}{81} = \frac{10}{81}$.

j. *Sample answer:* Because there are an odd number of possible outcomes, the game cannot be made perfectly fair. But by changing the operation to addition of the two integers, the probability of an even sum is $\frac{41}{81} \approx 0.506$.

k. *Sample answer:* You could make it less likely to spin an even product by making the area of the even triangles smaller than the odd.

Cumulative Test

1. a. central angle

     b. inscribed angle

     c. inscribed right angle

     d. inscribed angle

Answers

2. Given Circle C with center $(4, 3)$ and radius 3,

   Circle D with center $(1, 2)$ and radius 1

   Prove Circle C is similar to Circle D.

   Map Circle C to Circle C' by using the transformation $(x, y) \rightarrow (x - 3, y - 1)$ so that Circle C' and Circle D have the same center at $(1, 2)$. Dilate Circle C' using a center of dilation of $(1, 2)$ and a scale factor of $\frac{1}{3}$. Because there is a set of rigid transformations that maps Circle C to Circle D, Circle C is similar to Circle D.

3.

STATEMENTS	REASONS
1. $\angle A$ is supplementary to $\angle CDE$.	1. Given
2. $m\angle A + m\angle CDE = 180°$	2. Definition of supplementary angles
3. $m\angle A = 180° - m\angle CDE$	3. Subtraction Property of Equality
4. $m\angle BDE + m\angle CDE = 180°$	4. Definition of straight angles
5. $m\angle BDE = 180° - m\angle CDE$	5. Subtraction Property of Equality
6. $m\angle A = m\angle BDE$	6. Substitution
7. $\angle A \cong \angle BDE$	7. Definition of congruence
8. $\angle B \cong \angle B$	8. Identity
9. $\triangle ABC \sim \triangle DBE$	9. AA Similarity Theorem (Thm. 8.3)

4. C

5. $\overline{PQ}$ has a length of 6 units and a slope of 0; $\overline{RT}$ has a length of 6 units and a slope of 0; These opposite sides are congruent and parallel, so $PQRT$ is a parallelogram.

6. a. biconditional

   b. contrapositive

   c. converse

   d. inverse

7. yes; The opposite angles are supplementary, so the quadrilateral can be inscribed in a circle.

8. a. 90°

   b. 55°

   c. 80°

   d. 100°

9. a. triangle

   b. rectangle

10. $UP = VP$

11. D   **12.** B

13. The equation of the circle is $x^2 + y^2 = 18$. The point $(4, \sqrt{2})$ satisfies the equation, so the point $(4, \sqrt{2})$ lies on the circle.

14. $\dfrac{s\sqrt{\pi}}{\pi}$

15. yes; When the figure is rotated in the axis, the rectangular portion generates a cylinder and the triangular portion generates a cone.

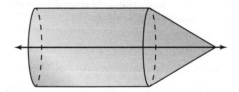

16. a.

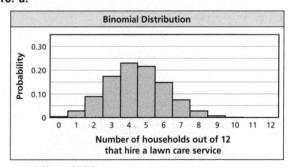

   b. 4 households

   c. $P(k \leq 6) \approx 0.89$

Answers

17. a.

		Class		
		Sign Language	French	Total
Gender	Female	33	19	52
	Male	21	22	43
	Total	54	41	95

  b. $P(\text{male and French}) = \frac{22}{95} \approx 0.232$

  c. $P(\text{sign language given Female}) = \frac{33}{52} \approx 0.635$

Post Course Test

1. 85 **2.** 28

3. $M(0.5, 2.5); D = \sqrt{130} \approx 11.4$ units

4. $K(8, 8); D = 6\sqrt{5} \approx 13.4$ units

5. true **6.** false **7.** false **8.** false

9. true **10.** false **11.** $x = 14$ **12.** $x = -1$

13. $x = 90$; Linear Pair Postulate (Post. 2.8), Alternate Exterior Angles Theorem (Thm. 3.3)

14. $y = 9$; Vertical Angles Congruence Theorem (Thm. 2.6), Consecutive Interior Angles Theorem (Thm. 3.4)

15. $x = 113$ **16.** $x = 27$

17. a. $y = -3x - 7$

  b. $y = \frac{1}{3}x - \frac{1}{3}$

18. a. $x = -3$

  b. $y = 1$

19. 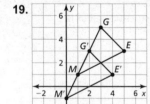 **20.**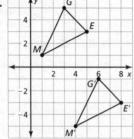

21.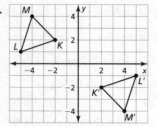

22.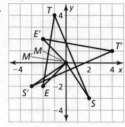

23. $m\angle A = 50°, m\angle B = 42°, m\angle ACB = 88°, m\angle ACD = 92°$

24. $m\angle D = 90°, m\angle E = 30°, m\angle F = 60°$

25. 16 **26.** 46

27. 45; Angle Bisector Theorem (Thm. 6.3)

28. 44; Perpendicular Bisector Theorem (Thm. 6.1)

29. $x = 36, y = 72$ **30.** $w = 6, z = 7$

31. rectangle; All four angles are 90°, but all four sides are not congruent.

32. parallelogram; Opposite sides are congruent, but there are no right angles.

33. yes; $\triangle BCA \sim \triangle EDF$

34. 3 **35.** 6

36. $a = 10.9, b = 6.1$ **37.** $c = 18.1, d = 19.7$

38. $AB = 19.2 , m\angle A = 51.3°, m\angle B = 38.7°$

39. $AC = 30.0$ m, $m\angle A = 30.0°, m\angle C = 32.0°$

40. $m\angle 1 = 74°$ **41.** $x = 3$

42. $x = 5$ **43.** $x = 4$

44. about 234.6 mi^3 **45.** 64 mi^3

46. about 105° **47.** about 183.3 m^2